nna sunderland

real life

surviving after education

ivp

Inter-Varsity Press

Inter-Varsity Press
38 De Montfort Street, Leicester LEI 7GP, England
Email: ivp@uccf.org.uk
Website: www.ivpbooks.com

© Joanna Sunderland 2005

Joanna Sunderland has asserted her right under the Copyright, Designs and Patents Act, 1988, to be identified as Author of this work.

All rights reserved. No part of this publication may be reproduced, stored in a retrieval system, or transmitted, in any form or by any means, electronic, mechanical, photocopying, recording or otherwise, without the prior permission of the publishers or the Copyright Licensing Agency.

Unless otherwise stated, Scripture quotations are from the Holy Bible, New International Version. Copyright © 1973, 1978, 1984 by International Bible Society. Used by permission of Hodder & Stoughton, a division of Hodder Headline Ltd. All rights reserved. 'NIV' is a registered trademark of International Bible Society. UK trademark number 1448790.

While every effort has been made to contact the copyright holders of all material used in this book, the publishers have not been successful in every case. Any amendment to these acknowledgments will gladly be incorporated in future printings.

First published 2005

British Library Cataloguing in Publication Data
A catalogue record for this book is available from the British Library.

ISBN-13: 978-1-84474-072-2
ISBN-10: 1-84474-072-2

Set in Monotype Dante 10.5/12.5pt
Typeset in Great Britain by CRB Associates, Reepham, Norfolk
Printed in Great Britain by Creative Print and Design (Wales), Ebbw Vale

Inter-Varsity Press is the publishing division of the Universities and Colleges Christian Fellowship (formerly the Inter-Varsity Fellowship), a student movement linking Christian Unions in universities and colleges throughout Great Britain, and a member movement of the International Fellowship of Evangelical Students. For more information about local and national activities write to UCCF, 38 De Montfort Street, Leicester LEI 7GP, email us at email@uccf.org.uk, or visit the UCCF website at www.uccf.org.uk.

Contents

	Foreword	6
	Introduction	8
1.	The final year	10
2.	What now?	22
3.	Unemployment – the big fear	30
4.	Who am I at work?	38
5.	Workplace issues	50
6.	A new place	64
7.	Money!	72
8.	Gap years	84
9.	Relationships	92
10.	Faith	106
	Postscript: A confession	115
	For further thought . . .	117

Dedicated to Tim who encouraged me to write

I said to the man
Who stood at the gate of the year
'Give me a light that I may tread safely
into the unknown.'
And he replied,
'Go into the darkness
and put your hand into the hand of God
That shall be to you
Better than light
And safer than a known way!'
So I went forth
and finding the hand of God
Trod gladly into the night
He led me towards the hills
And the breaking of day in the lone east.
So heart be still!
What need our human life to know
If God hath comprehension?
In all the dizzy strife of things
Both high and low,
God hideth his intention.

Minnie Haskins (d. 1957), 'The Gate of the Year'

Foreword

Joanna Sunderland is one of life's rare creatures. She is not only a survivor herself, but is also self-aware and able to retrace the steps of her own journey from university to the workplace. More than that, she has a passionate concern for the survival of her fellow travellers. By drawing on her own recent experiences of graduation, employment and marriage, Joanna is able to empathize as well as advise as she lays out simple, practical and godly advice to readers who have just started on this journey.

The survival guide begins with the last year of university/college, helping the student reader make practical plans for revision, rest and spiritual growth. It then charts the choppy waters of returning home and facing unemployment, before taking you into its main territory of the world of work.

It is very easy for twenty-first-century Christians to go to one of two extremes. Either we unquestioningly embrace a Protestant work ethic that seems to suggest that the harder and more successfully we work then the greater our Christian witness will be, or we are tempted to see work as a necessary evil that puts food on the table and full-time Christian workers on the mission field.

Joanna refreshingly refuses to go to either route. Her emphasis is on God being interested in every aspect of our lives, which include relationships, money, time, ambition, sexual purity, honesty and guidance. Such a holistic and practical emphasis chimes with the famous words of the Dutch Prime Minister Abraham Kuyper: 'There is not one square inch of the entire creation about which Jesus Christ does not cry out, "This is mine! This belongs to me!"'

Real Life often reads like a journal. It is a generous, personal and warm-hearted guide to all students who wish to keep God first in those precarious early months and years after graduation. I warmly commend it not only to students, but also to fellow parents and Christian workers.

Richard Cunningham
Director UCCF (The Christian Unions)
January 2005

Introduction

People say school days are the best days of your life; for me it was my years at Leeds University. I had so many friends, so much support and now so many memories. But as we walk through life, we have to carry on growing up and I started the grown-up world of work kicking and screaming, wishing I could carry on being a student for ever.

This book is designed to give you inspiration and hope when things are tough. It is a reminder to dream, to remember those midnight conversations about setting the world to rights and believe you can still do it.

From day one, when you leave formal education behind, you have the ability to make a difference; often it won't feel like it, but with your hand in the hand of God you can tread safely into the unknown and he will provide a path for you to walk on.

There may be brambles and briars on the way, steep and scary slopes, easy diversions and distractions, but my prayer for you is that you carry on walking through it all and become the whole person God made you to be.

There have been many times in my life when I have wanted to fast-forward the stage I was going through or stop, curl up in a ball and refuse to move on. But time never stops and with the loving help of my family, friends and heavenly Maker I hope I am now slightly more like the person God made me to be.

This book has been written out of my own personal struggle; out of my doubts about God, my frustrations with work, my loneliness and isolation in a big city. It has been written remembering the good times and refusing to live in a world of memories but to carry on walking forward. It has been teased and tangled out in collaboration with many friends who have shared their stories with me as we have tried to piece together the puzzles of direction, ambition, faith and, ultimately, life.

I could never have written this book by myself and want to thank all those friends and acquaintances who didn't mind filling in questionnaires and letting me 'steal' their stories to illustrate this book.

Many of the issues covered in this book are not directly related to leaving full-time education but to leaving childhood and adolescence behind in general. Hopefully, by addressing some of the issues, we will not only get older but will get older graciously!

chapter 1

the final year

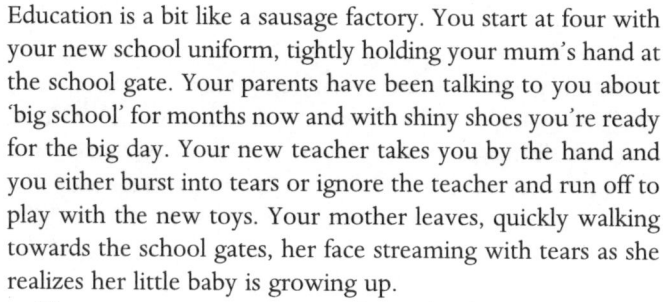

Education is a bit like a sausage factory. You start at four with your new school uniform, tightly holding your mum's hand at the school gate. Your parents have been talking to you about 'big school' for months now and with shiny shoes you're ready for the big day. Your new teacher takes you by the hand and you either burst into tears or ignore the teacher and run off to play with the new toys. Your mother leaves, quickly walking towards the school gates, her face streaming with tears as she realizes her little baby is growing up.

Then comes stage two: secondary school. Now if you're a bit cooler, your mum won't be with you. Probably she walked with you to the bus stop where you looked embarrassed but actually desperately wanted her to be there. In your brand-new school uniform you get on the bus and your stomach aches with fear. You look around, wondering where to sit. At the back, four older girls with their ties tied around their waist and their skirts hitched to reveal most of their thighs take up approximately two rows each. You opt for the front row; maybe the driver will protect you?

Before you know it, your GCSEs have come and gone and you're onto A levels. Your teachers are encouraging you to go

real life | the final year

to university or college and it seems like a good idea to get away from home and your annoying kid sister. A few application forms and it's all in the bag. Well, you didn't get your first choice, but you only applied to Oxbridge because your parents wanted you to – huh?

And there we have it. Before you know it you're at the end of the government's target education programme. Most of your life has been spent in preparation for this new world – the world of work. Something you will have to do for the next forty or so years – and that's if they don't raise the age of retirement. Looking back, you may have often been told what to do but not always why. Now it's time to work it out for yourself.

From the start of his ministry Jesus began preparing his disciples for the time when he would leave them, rather like education prepares us for work. Jesus taught them in small group sessions as well as large, open gatherings. They lived together, sleeping in the same room, eating meals together and sharing a common purse. But when Jesus was taken away and crucified, the disciples panicked. Simon Peter cut off a soldier's ear and then a few hours later denied Jesus. The rest of the disciples fled, scared and confused; wasn't Jesus meant to be the Messiah? When Jesus left, the disciples didn't feel very prepared. They were hiding in a room with the door firmly locked when Jesus appeared to them and said 'Peace be with you' (John 20:19). However, over time and with the help of the Holy Spirit they learned to adapt to life without Jesus. They learned to do things for themselves and became bold in preaching the gospel – the work Jesus had called them to do. Like the disciples, many students leaving full-time education can feel a bit lost and confused. Starting to prepare yourself for the transition in the final year of education can be really helpful in bridging the gap between student days and working life.

Making time to think
'When I left college I had no idea of what I wanted to do. I had done an English degree and worried that actually it was a complete waste of time. While I applied for "serious" jobs I got a temping job. I seemed to spend all my time trying to get enough money to pay my bills and rent and didn't have the time to keep looking for jobs and filling in application forms. I was working rubbish hours for rubbish pay and was really fed up. After a year and a half I moved to cheaper accommodation and started to work part-time so I could get out the negative cycle I had got myself stuck in.'

When Jesus was about thirty he stopped following the family trade of carpentry and changed career direction. All his life he had been waiting for this opportunity and now it was time to start his new life doing his Father's work. He would be travelling away from family and friends to new places and new situations. But before it all began, Jesus spent forty days in the desert preparing for his new job (see Matthew 4). This was a time when he fasted and prayed and gave himself space to think before facing the new challenge ahead.

As you move on to a new phase in your life, try following Jesus' example. Making time to stop and pray in your final year of education will help you feel more prepared for a life of work ahead. It may not feel as if you have much time now, but you'll probably have more time before you finish education than you will afterwards.

What experience do you need to get a job?
As you stop and think, ask yourself 'What skills do I need to get a job?' Your final year may be the last opportunity to do some voluntary work or collect some experience to make your CV stand out above the rest.

'In my final year of university I decided to write for the student paper. It was relevant to my degree but something I had never done before. Soon I was given my first assignment. Working on the paper gave me confidence, which stood me in good stead when I went looking for a job. I think it was the confidence rather than the experience that got me my first job, although my employer was impressed with it on my CV.'

You don't have to try to do everything; even one little thing can make a big difference. Pray for guidance about what to invest your time in, and plan your workload so that you can keep to the commitments you have made and also have fun!

Consolidate friendships

During your years in education you may have had people around you who have supported you, mentored you, or just been good friends. Maybe a friend from back home or a person in your church has prayed for you every week. Take time out to encourage those people and tell them you appreciate them before you get too busy.

If you have a really close friendship-group from university or college start consolidating your relationships with them. Learn to be accountable to each other by talking through decisions together and sharing any areas of life that you struggle with. Often the first few weeks of your final year are the lull before the storm. Then it's essays, dissertations, exams and, before you know it, you and your best friend may be at opposite sides of the country in new jobs and new places, struggling to find your feet. If you want to still be in touch with people when you're drawing your pension, start investing in your relationships when they live two doors down instead of two hundred miles away.

> ***Tips on creating strong relationships:***
> - Support each other and see each other especially when other people around you are stressed.
> - Be accountable to each other, not just for the present but long-term.
> - Give them a list of questions to ask you about things you struggle with.
> - Get used to praying together.

'After college you lose touch with your friends so quickly, even those you are sure will be best friends forever start drifting away. There's only time to see so many people and when you're scattered all over the country you have to be realistic about who to keep in touch with.'

By creating strong relationships now maybe you won't share the regrets voiced by one ex-student:

'A lot of friends from university, including those who served on the Christian Union exec., are no longer Christians. We rarely talk about God. Sometimes I wonder what we could have done differently to stop them falling away. Maybe if everyone had been paired up in a close accountable relationship they would still be Christians today.'

An example of strong friendship in the Bible is the relationship between Jonathan and David (1 Samuel 23:18). Many times Jonathan's dad Saul tried to kill David, but God let David escape. On one occasion when King Saul told Jonathan that he was going to kill David, Jonathan interceded for him. He stood in the gap between his father and his friend and reminded Saul that David hadn't actually done anything wrong; in fact, he had defeated Goliath and saved the people of Israel.

Later Jonathan protected David by telling him to stay away from the 'New Moon' meal where Saul was again planning to kill him. Using a coded message he told David to go far away where Saul could not find him.

Jonathan and David had what has been called a covenant friendship. This is a special relationship based on shared promises; they promised they would always love and protect each other and each other's family. In today's world where we move from place to place for work and study, often discarding friendships and relationships as we go, we need to learn to keep our promises.

Recently I went to a screening of a film made by four homeless men from West Yorkshire. Three out of the four were made homeless by relationship breakdowns. They were living on the streets because they had no-one to turn to. At the end of the film one man gave a speech and said: 'If we want to change the world we need to turn off the telly and start looking out for each other instead.'

We need to be friends that will be there in times of difficulty. You may have just spent three years with people and know them really well. Is there one person you can promise to support even if the going gets really tough?

Have fun!
Make the most of your last year in education. When you leave you may have more money but you will definitely have less time; while you've got the time, enjoy it.

If you're going to be leaving the area where you studied go and visit those places near by that are classed as not-to-be-missed 'tourist attractions'. If you haven't got the time at the moment, set a date for a day out and get all your mates to mark it in their diary too. Life always seems better when you have something to look forward to!

'One of my regrets from university is not going to the final graduation ball. On one hand it was definitely a waste of money, but if I could go back, I would have liked to have been there. I think the end of your student days marks a particular rite of passage. It's something to celebrate, but also something to mourn as you realize life will never be the same again.'

Don't miss those last student moments of madness; you can never go back to them.

Think about where you are going to live
'By the time I stopped being a student most of my friends were from church. I really think that helped me make the transition from student life to adult life. It gave me people to hang around with while I looked for a job.'

Consider where you might live. If you do want to stay in your current city or town, think about making new friends. Two years after I graduated my last close friend from university moved away. Most of them had left immediately after graduation. (In chapter 2 I look more fully at the question of whether to go home or stay put.) Your final year is a great time to get plugged in to new activities and church life, so that when your mates do move on you still know people and have an active social life!

Living under stress
The last few months of any course are always stressful. Here are some tips on how to keep calm.

Work by yourself

Stress is catching. As the only arts student in a house of seven final year students I can prove it! Even if I had done all my planned revision and my essays were on target, I only had to talk to some of my housemates to feel stressed and guilty about the amount of work I was doing.

Work by yourself, keep to your plan and ignore everybody else's. Asking other people how their work is going rarely makes you feel better. Use the library and don't work next to your mates. Sitting with people you don't know, who aren't going to ask you to answer a question you'd never even considered before – sending both you and them into a panic trying to solve it – is crucial for concentration.

Take time off

Make sure you take time off. Bribe yourself to work an extra half-an-hour in return for a proper lunch-break. Go outside and count the clouds, see how many stairs you can run up or buy a newspaper. Plan afternoons or evenings off. You will work more effectively when you have scheduled fun time. God created days off, so they must be important.

Establish a routine

Don't stop your quiet times because you think that extra ten minutes of sleep is more important. Similarly don't stop eating or cooking. The twenty minutes it takes to boil some pasta and make dinner is probably an essential rest time for your brain.

Don't forget that your exams and all this stress aren't going to last for ever. Get the maximum amount of sympathy from your family while you can.

Don't envy
Finally, be happy at others' success. If your friend lands a dream job, don't be jealous. Most people don't get a job before they've even sat their finals. Remember you're not in a minority, there is still lots of time left.

real life | the final year

In brief

Before your exams
Make time to think.
Get relevant experience.
Consider where you will and won't live.
Consolidate friendships and set up prayer and accountability partners.

During your exams
Don't stress.
Work hard, rest hard.
Establish a routine.
Don't panic at what your friends are doing.
Be pleased for others' success.

Further reading
<http://www.graduateimpact.com>.
A host of articles and practical advice with a biblical perspective on life as a graduate.
<http://www.uccf.org.uk/graduates>.
Lots of links to specific professional groups for Christian support and advice.

chapter 2

what now?

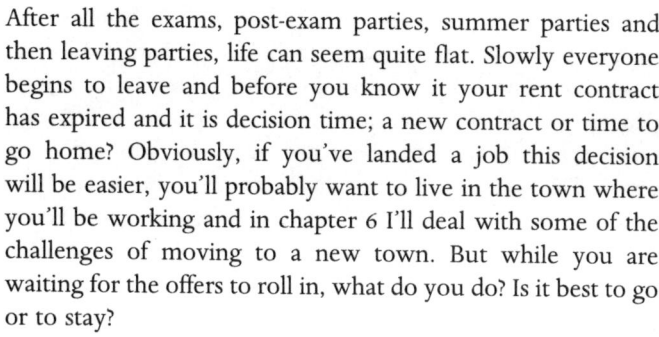

After all the exams, post-exam parties, summer parties and then leaving parties, life can seem quite flat. Slowly everyone begins to leave and before you know it your rent contract has expired and it is decision time; a new contract or time to go home? Obviously, if you've landed a job this decision will be easier, you'll probably want to live in the town where you'll be working and in chapter 6 I'll deal with some of the challenges of moving to a new town. But while you are waiting for the offers to roll in, what do you do? Is it best to go or to stay?

Returning home
If you have a good relationship with your family, going home can seem like a good idea: clean sheets, nice meals and often no rent or bills to pay. It can seem like heaven after student squalor. However, returning home can have its problems too, for while you see yourself as several years older and wiser, your family still see the eighteen-year-old who left home without knowing how to use a washing machine. Suddenly no-one knows how to treat each other anymore.

There are three ways this new relationship with your family

real life | what now?

can go; you can clash, regress or get on. For most people it's a mixture of all three.

Clashing

'I found it hard to return home after university. I had changed a lot while I was away and now had quite a different view of the world from my father. If we didn't ignore this we would constantly argue about it. I spent a lot of time working and seeing friends to avoid being in the house.'

24

The book of Acts tells the story of the early Christian church. Jesus has gone back to heaven and the disciples are preaching their hearts out. People are getting healed, new believers are joining their community daily, people are sharing all their possessions and living in harmony; then suddenly it all goes pear-shaped. There is an argument between the Jewish and Greek-speaking widows about the allocation of food (Acts 6:1–6). This issue could have split the fragile community of the new church in two. The Greek and Jewish believers could have formed two separate sides, one side arguing, 'It always happens like this. You Jews think you are so superior, you won't even give us enough to eat,' and the other side muttering, 'You Greeks are always complaining. You want more than your fair share ... ' Soon the issue wouldn't be about food – all the old jealousies and bitterness would surface and the argument would escalate. And that's how it can be when you go back home.

You may have almost forgotten the days of teenage arguments with your family, but in the stress of re-adjusting to a post-student life sometimes old issues get brought up again. You may think you are a completely different person from the naïve eighteen-year-old who left home with her teddy bear hidden in the bottom of her bag – God's done loads of stuff with you over the last few years. And you've got used to living with people who treated you as an adult. It was your decision when to come home, when to go out and what to eat for dinner. Suddenly all that changes. The old argument comes up again. It doesn't matter what it is about – before you know it they are no longer treating you like an adult, they're treating you like a kid.

You can feel like you are still trying to act grown-up but it doesn't seem to work. Nothing is getting through and finally you feel like running up the stairs, slamming the door of your room and shouting 'I wish I'd never come home.'

Regressing

'I wasn't really prepared for post-student life. All my life I had been in structured education and now there was no natural progression. At university I had this great community, but suddenly at the end of term it all disappeared around me. There was no-one and no reason to stay around, so I went home, back to my parents.

'Suddenly I was back in the same bedroom I had lived in since I was seven. I wandered around not knowing what to do with myself. My mum looked after me and I had no independence left. I regressed into being a moody teenager again.'

The trouble is that however much your parents want to see you as an adult, they probably find it hard to see you as much older than a kid. Last year I went to visit one of my friends and her family. Her older brother was at home and was proudly showing off how his new baby son could walk. As he sat down he knocked over a small coffee table and was told off by his dad. To me he was the epitome of a 'proper grown up', but to his dad he was just a big kid!

When I was at university my sisters and I were always fairly grown-up until it got to Christmas. A combination of not enough sleep (three of us sharing one room), the excitement and all of us being together again generally made us a little hyper. It would start with us yelling to each other up and down the house: 'Have you any wrapping paper?', followed by 'Can't hear you'. That would be enough to kill the peaceful atmosphere and drive my mum mad. We might have sung the carol, 'Silent night ... all is calm, all is bright', but it definitely wasn't silent or calm at home.

Life hasn't changed much. Last year my sister still banged on my bedroom door at 7am on Christmas morning to tell me and my husband to open our stockings. Sometimes it's hard to be an adult at home, but it often helps family harmony.

Getting on

When the disciples heard about the complaints from the Greek widows they didn't ignore the problem and bury their heads in the sand; they decided to do something about it. Choosing people to oversee the problem, they gave them the authority to make decisions, prayed for them and left them to it. It was still an issue, it hadn't been resolved yet but they had dedicated time and resources into getting the problem sorted. Moving back home after living away for a few years is going to bring inevitable tensions. These won't go away if you don't address them. Tackle each problem head on. Don't allow it to fester or to deteriorate into a situation where the fact that you shaved your eyebrows off at sixteen and ruined your sister's wedding gets dragged up too.

If you are planning on being at home for several months rather than a few weeks, it's a good idea to have a chat with your family about their expectations and your expectations. They might not be the same!

'Before I came home from university I asked whether my girlfriend was allowed upstairs? It was the norm in our halls but never allowed before I left home. I also asked my parents about what they expected of me? My mum said I could have my girlfriend in my room, so we could have somewhere private to talk, and told me to do

my own washing. Within two weeks of being at home my dad told me he had changed his mind about my girlfriend and my mum said she would do my washing because I was messing up her system!'

Parents make funny decisions; that's their prerogative as you come back and live in their house which they have had to themselves for the last few years. As you return home, it is your responsibility to react to those decisions as an adult and not revert back to being a child.

When you're tired, fed up and missing your mates it's easy to take it out on your family. Ask your friends to hold you accountable in your family relationships and don't retreat to moody-teenager mode.

Moving on: don't get stuck

Many students go home after university simply because they don't know what to do next. One student explains his situation when he had three months at home with no job:

'It was great to be home and see my family again but I was bored out of my skull and had little incentive to go and find a job. The problem was I didn't have to pay rent so I didn't need much money and therefore I wasn't in a hurry to get anything done. With no external discipline I soon started to get up late, go to bed late and use the time badly. It was only getting a job that got me out of this pattern. Looking back, if I'd have known I had three months at home and a job at the end, I could have enjoyed it enormously.'

Hindsight; what a wonderful thing! If you lack motivation, it's worth considering whether you really do want to move back home. Maybe you and a mate could do a house swap and pay rent to each other's parents if you both want to return to your home town but not necessarily your own parents.

In the Bible Jesus did tell some people to go back to their communities and share what God had done for them. Legion, a guy plagued by demons, was healed by Jesus. He told him specifically to return to his house and tell his neighbours what great things God has done (Luke 8:39).

God may call you to return to where you have come from and live a life that shows what he has done for you while you have been away at university. Return as an adult whether you live at home or not. Timothy writes, 'Don't let anyone look down on you because you are young, but set an example' (1 Timothy 4:12). It's not easy to set an example; you're not alone.

Staying put

Whatever happens after university is a step of faith, but deciding to stay in the same city with no job and limiting your opportunities by that decision definitely calls for some trust in God. (The next chapter looks at unemployment.)

There are many good reasons to stay around in your university city; maybe you want to give something back to the community or perhaps you've put down roots there. A bad reason to stay is because you want things to be the same. They won't be. If you stay you'll have to grow up, life doesn't stay still.

'When I left university I got involved in youth work. It was a great way of getting to know people with a similar outlook to me who were part of the city I had chosen to live in. It made me feel much more at home and less like a student who hadn't yet moved away.'

Using contacts with other Christians and students, consider whether you could mentor someone who is in their final year. Find time to get involved in the community around you. If you feel you haven't got time to get involved when you first leave full-time education, you'll be unlikely to make time later.

In brief

If returning home
Talk to your family before you go home about your expectations and theirs.
Return as an adult.
Try to reason like an adult even if you feel your family aren't treating you like one.
Don't revert back to being a moody teenager – talk to your family when you get home.
Don't get stuck, carry on growing up.

If staying where you've been studying
Get to know people who aren't students. Consider voluntary work or local community projects.
Don't try to carry on being a student.
Consider mentoring someone through his or her final year at university.

unemployment – the big fear

chapter 3

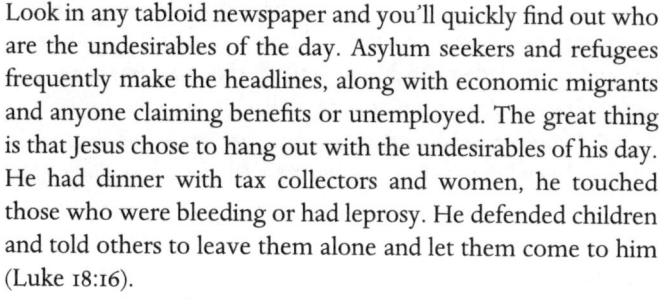

Look in any tabloid newspaper and you'll quickly find out who are the undesirables of the day. Asylum seekers and refugees frequently make the headlines, along with economic migrants and anyone claiming benefits or unemployed. The great thing is that Jesus chose to hang out with the undesirables of his day. He had dinner with tax collectors and women, he touched those who were bleeding or had leprosy. He defended children and told others to leave them alone and let them come to him (Luke 18:16).

In one of Jesus' parables (found in Matthew 25:14–30), a king went to his servants and gave them money to invest while he was away. Many years later he came back to his kingdom, called his servants to him and asked what they had done with the money. The first servant had been given five talents of money and had invested it well, earning five more talents. The next servant had also doubled the money he'd been given, but the third dug up his from the ground, returned it to his master and said, 'I was afraid and went out and hid your talent in the ground. See, here is what belongs to you.' The king rewarded the first two servants, but to the third he said, 'You wicked, lazy servant! . . . You should have put my money on deposit . . .

so that when I returned I would have received it back with interest.'

Being unemployed does not mean you have to put your life on hold. It may be a difficult period, but you can still use the talents and time God has given you while unemployed. He has many more plans for you than just getting a job.

After I graduated I spent six weeks unemployed. Six weeks isn't really all that long, but at the time it felt like an eternity. I'd gone from being busy and having loads of mates around to complete and utter boredom. Suddenly I had no reason to get up in the morning. An extract from my journal says:

It's another day with nothing to do. I write a list to try and plan something to do in the ten hours I'm here by myself. Going to bed late and getting up late is the only way to squeeze a few more hours of human contact into the day. I can no longer live life as though I am busy. Those around me who are lonely and depressed, those I like and those I don't, I have time for them now. I am one of them.

I live for the weekends. Two days of company and then five days alone again. I grasp at straws. I don't want to get involved in any committed volunteering opportunities, instead I sit by the phone convinced it will ring soon. Sitting in waiting for a call, getting up early only to check the post before returning to bed, waiting, waiting, waiting ...

Unemployment can be a lonely place, the uncertainty of not knowing how much longer you have to wait, the hopeless despair of waiting for letters that bring only rejection or for a promised phone-call that is never made. This is a time when you most need to trust in God and remind yourself where you have come from and where you are going. It's not easy and often needs to be done on an hourly basis.

Arguing with God
'When I was unemployed I asked God why? I knew he had wanted me to do my degree, so why couldn't I get a job at the end of it? It just didn't seem to make sense.'

It's okay to question God and ask 'why?' Look at the psalms, they are full of people crying out to God and asking 'why?' (e.g. Psalms 10; 13; 22; 30 and 74). They presented their pain and confusion and in it found peace. We often need to pray through our pain and confusion to the stage when we can honestly stand before God and say 'I don't understand it but your will not mine.'

You may have stayed on in education by default: perhaps it was expected of you by your family, or it was easier than getting a job? You might not have been a Christian or you might not have asked God for his opinion, it doesn't matter – God used it to shape your life. Look back over that time and ask yourself when God has spoken to you about your life. Maybe it was through a conversation with a course tutor: did he or she suggest something or affirm you in something that resonated with who you thought you might be? Maybe God spoke to you through a random thought, hymn or sunset? Think about what God has told you about your future. What have other people told you about your gifts and abilities? Write them all down, then take them to God and ask, 'Where do you want me to go now?'

When I was unemployed I found it really useful to 'paint' prayers. Using dark colours I'd paint my despair, confusion and rejection, giving it to God. Using newspapers I'd make collage sentences explaining how I was feeling. Then I would pray as it all dried, reminding myself of what God has promised; that he would always love me, protect me, comfort me and provide for me. I'd write these over the paint in chalk. Through the slow process I'd be able to express my anger to God, calm down and give him time to respond to me.

No matter how it may feel, you are not alone when struggling with unemployment. There is someone bigger than you to whom you can hold on. God has a plan for your life. Isaiah reminds us that we don't see the whole picture, God's plans are bigger and better than ours:

> As the heavens are higher than the earth,
>   so are my ways higher than your ways,
> and my thoughts than your thoughts.
> (Isaiah 55:9)

Rejection

'As I left university I decided not to panic. My motto is now to live life in small chunks. You don't have to decide what to do for the next twenty-five years, just decide what to do for the next year or maybe the year after that. Life is made up of lots of small chunks. When you're looking for a job or moving to a new place, just concentrate on one chunk at a time.'

In Western society we tend to define people by their job description. The question 'What do you do?' is asked so often. Yet in other parts of the world people are defined by their family. They are known as 'Son of so-and-so' or 'Mother of so-and-so'. We are 'Children of God' and no matter how many rejection letters you get, God never rejects you. God delights in you and takes pleasure in you.

Being rejected so many times can make you doubt who you are. But as Christians we need to know where we get our worth from and give to God our feelings of inadequacy and rejection. You are worth more than the sum total of your job.

Unemployment – not just a negative

'I was unemployed for a year after university and volunteered for an Oxfam depot sorting out clothes before they got sent to charity shops. It was fab, one of the best things I have done.

'The people were more real and interesting than those I had left at university. They were not obsessed with what "graduates" worry excessively about: jobs, houses and partners. They were much more settled and content with life, which was what I really needed and got me out of the normal ex-student loop.'

Unemployment doesn't have to undermine your confidence, it can build it up, especially if you use the time to gain new skills and meet new people. Unemployment can teach you a lot about yourself and God and how to work together in partnership. As the Bible says: 'In all your ways acknowledge him, and he will make your paths straight' (Proverbs 3:6).

But if you are finding it tough, remember, something will come up eventually and even if it's not exactly what you wanted, God can still use it. Just as he will have used the process you went through to get it.

real life | unemployment – the big fear

In brief

Trust in God.
It's okay to ask God 'why?'
Remember what God has promised to you.
God never rejects you.
Don't define yourself by your job description.
Use your time wisely.

Further reading
What colour is your parachute? Richard Nelson-Bolles (Ten Speed Press, rev. 2003).

37

chapter 4

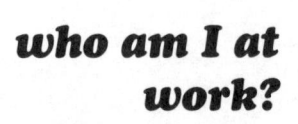

who am I at work?

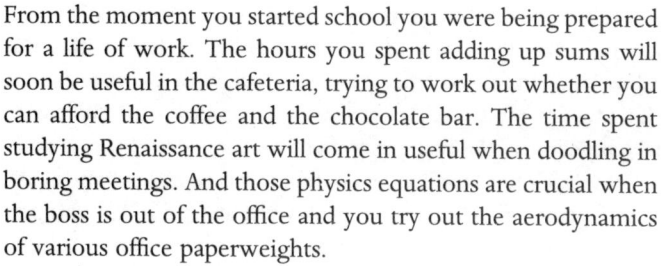

From the moment you started school you were being prepared for a life of work. The hours you spent adding up sums will soon be useful in the cafeteria, trying to work out whether you can afford the coffee and the chocolate bar. The time spent studying Renaissance art will come in useful when doodling in boring meetings. And those physics equations are crucial when the boss is out of the office and you try out the aerodynamics of various office paperweights.

David, son of Jesse, didn't work in an office; he looked after his family's sheep. He was the youngest of eight and was always left the menial work, taking food and drink to his brothers who were in the army and carrying messages for people, scurrying here, there and everywhere for his father. The Israelites were fighting the Philistines in the Valley of Elah, but instead of the usual fighting, the Philistines had challenged the Israelites to a dual. One man would fight their champion, Goliath, and the side that lost would become slaves to the winners. The stalemate had been going on for forty days when David heard the cry and decided to do something about it. David was incensed with the Philistines' taunts against 'the armies of the living God' (1 Samuel 17:26) and volunteered to fight the giant.

To everyone else David was a little shepherd boy, but from his own perspective he was a child of God who was used to fighting animals to protect his sheep and who believed that God would help him fight Goliath. At work you need to decide who you are going to be. Often a new job is the chance to start again; people don't know who you are, they don't know your past behaviour or your family. You can decide who you want to be and by putting your hand in the hand of God you can, together, go out and fight giants.

When David went onto the battlefield, he went in the name of God, saying, 'You come against me with sword and spears and javelin, but I come against you in the name of the LORD Almighty, the God of the armies of Israel' (1 Samuel 17:45). Work can be a battlefield and it's important to go in there with God. When someone asks you what you did with your weekend, don't be ashamed to tell them you went to church; it's a lot easier to tell people at the beginning than five years down the line.

Work is a new challenge; it's fun, exciting and can motivate you enormously. You may never have managed to get yourself out of bed before 12, let alone made sure you shave and cut your hair regularly, but some unknown boss may provide just the inspiration you need to be transformed from a scruffy student into a pinstriped executive. You may be the lowest in your office or the newest in the place of work, but you have a job title that sounds impressive and wait until your mates see your business cards!

However, it can also be hard work and at times can leave you feeling frustrated and out of your depth. Office politics and company expectations can often affect you more than the 'real' work you have to do. Politics can just be so complicated! How were you meant to know that it was impossible to be friends with those two groups of people? An argument twenty years ago and they're still not speaking now!

A lot of work is about teamwork, working with people, accepting their limitations and letting them accept yours. This means being honest. No-one is perfect and at the end of a long stressful day it doesn't take much for people to get on your nerves. Chapters 4 and 5 are about the issues that affect everyone at work, from the managing director to the office junior, looking at where the pressures come from and how to get a good work–life balance. Work to live, don't live to work!

Why work?

There will always be times when you don't feel like working. Maybe you're coming down with the flu or stayed up too late the night before? It's good to remind yourself why we work and why God sees it as important.

God calls us to work. The Bible opens in Genesis with God working. He created the world, the heavens, the universe, man and beast and took pleasure in what he did. God saw work as a good thing. God then asked Adam to look after the Garden of Eden, to care for it and take responsibility for it (Genesis 2:15). God gave Adam purpose in life in giving him 'work' to enjoy.

When you're struggling with work, read Psalm 90. It is thought to have been written by Moses as the older generation of Israelites was dying out in the desert. The community knew they would be unable to enter the Promised Land until all of the last generation had gone. They were a community waiting for time to pass and then they could re-enter the Promised Land and live out their inheritance. Yet in those times, times when they felt in limbo, times when they were unsure of the future ahead, they cried out to God and asked him to bless their work. The Psalm pleads:

real life | who am I at work?

> May the favour of the Lord our God rest upon us;
>   establish the work of our hands for us –
>   yes, establish the work of our hands.
> (Psalm 90:17)

It was a prayer asking for significance and value to be added to the work they were doing. They didn't want to die in vain; they wanted what they were doing to make a difference, even though it was a temporary time in a temporary place.

Paul uses the same theology of work in writing to the Corinthians: 'Therefore, my dear brothers, stand firm. Let nothing move you. Always give yourselves fully to the work of the Lord, because you know that your work in the Lord is not in vain' (1 Corinthians 15:58). Whatever work we do, whether it is 'Christian work' or secular work, God wants you to do it well, he sees the worth in it. Believe that the work you do makes a difference and that God is pleased with it.

Know who you are at work

Start off by knowing who you are in God. Who has he called you to be? What has he asked you to do? Do you feel your job is the principal thing God has called you to do in life, or do you look at it as a way to pay the bills?

In the Bible different people viewed their work in different ways. It didn't matter to God, he communicated with each one individually in their own situation.

Take Moses as an example. You can read about his early life in Exodus 2 – 4. He was a shepherd. As a young man he had lived in the royal palace of Pharaoh, until his anger and uncontrolled temper got the better of him and he had to run away. He was now a long way from his own history and people, but he wasn't far away from God.

God specifically called Moses to lead his people out of Egypt into the Promised Land. It was his vocation and calling. It wasn't a nine-to-five job, it was something that controlled his whole life and being.

At the other end of the scale, in the midst of a famine a widow called Ruth went to the harvest fields to gather leftover grain so that she and her mother-in-law wouldn't starve. (You can read her story in the book of Ruth.) I'm sure working in the full heat of the day, trying to keep away from men who might take advantage of her, she didn't thank God for discovering his calling on her life. I'm sure she asked God why she had no husband and no sons to provide for her. Her work was a way to bring bread to the table, but she served God and her mother-in-law diligently and God was pleased with her and blessed her with a new husband and a son.

Whatever you do, whether you are on the first step towards your dream career, or if things haven't worked out quite as you planned, it doesn't matter. God is with you and he believes in you.

Write your own vision statement

One of the best ways to motivate yourself about your work is to write your own vision statement. Decide what is important to you about your job, pray about it, then try to live it.

Before you start a new job or in the first few weeks of work decide what you want to get out of it. What are your goals and plans? Don't let someone else decide how you are going to approach the forty hours a week that are taken up with work, decide for yourself first. Write a vision statement and stick it up on your desk. Now this may seem a fairly silly idea after applying for a job with a specific job description, but it does make a difference to how you view your job.

First of all, it makes you consider what your job is for. Is it purely for man's purposes or is it also for God's purposes? A few months after I started in my current job I wrote a vision statement and looking back I am amazed how much of what I wanted to incorporate into my job has now become part of what I do.

My vision statement
- To highlight injustice and social exclusion.
- To campaign for justice and give people a platform from which to speak.
- To help build a community and stabilize the area racially and culturally.
- To be righteous in my work, relationships and responsibility.
- To provide breathing space, thinking space and play space in an inner-city context.
- To be like Jesus to those around me.

It's not easy to emulate a vision statement and mine is about what I want to do and be, rather than how I am and what I do. However, by having it I get challenged to look for God's purposes in situations rather than just concentrating on my own agenda.

A good vision statement helps you believe you can make a difference in your place of work. How you do your work can make more of a difference to your colleagues around you than what work you do.

I work in a newsroom and there have been times when a big story has broken and suddenly the office is filled with senior reporters I have never met in my life transmitting stress around the office. The pressure for them to get an exclusive interview before the competition is immense, but the way they go about getting the story doesn't only affect them it affects the whole office, it affects me!

What you do in your work and the ways you carry out your work can really make a difference. There will always be times of stress but give them to God and let him deal with them, then do as much as you can. Actions speak louder than words.

Decide your own value-system

Decide how you are going to live at work, before you get into a situation where you aren't sure what to do. Think through some basic questions about work and potential circumstances. What will you go home for? How often will you work weekends? Does truth matter more than promotion? Will you lie for your boss? The list is endless.

Jesus calls us to live with integrity, but deception and falsehood are all around us whether we choose to lie, or whether someone else does.

'I had only been in the office a few days and yet another technical problem had come up with the software I was using. I had spent the last half an hour fiddling with the program, changing the settings, altering the password, but whatever I did, it just wasn't going to work.

'My colleague looked up. "Why don't you phone Dave?" he said. I hesitated. I'd never met this person and it would be the third time this week I had phoned him to ask his advice. The solution was always so simple. Well simple when you knew what to do . . .

'I picked up the phone and dialled the number. "It's ringing", I said, looking across the desk at my colleague eating his sandwiches. He replied "Don't tell him I'm in." As I opened my mouth to respond, Dave picks up the phone. I put on my most charming voice, apologized profusely and sure enough within five minutes it was fixed. Thanking him, I was about to end the conversation when he asked: "Is Mark in?"'

real life | who am I at work?

It's always hard to know what to say when people ask you to lie for them. Whether it is about an invoice in the post or fobbing off a client, bending the truth or telling white lies, it can quickly lead you down a path of deception, where people start to expect you to lie for them on a regular basis.

Thinking about your response in advance can help you in those awkward moments when you have a split second to respond and you open your mouth without really knowing what is going to come out.

Mark Greene's book, *Thank God it's Monday: Ministry in the workplace*, shares a story of what happens when a secretary refuses to lie (page 154):

> Janette Taylor works as a secretary in a military establishment, the kind of place where an order is an order and you expect to be obeyed. She is a civilian, but she works in a command culture.
>
> The phone rings. It's her boss. She tells him that so-and-so is on the line. He says, as do thousands of people all over Britain everyday, 'Tell him I'm out.'
>
> Janette says, 'I can't do that. You're not.'
>
> There is a pause.
>
> She continues, 'If I lie for you, you won't know when I'm lying to you.'

Another example of someone refusing to go with the status quo is Daniel, a character from the Old Testament who had nerves of steel and principles to match. His name means 'God is my judge' and that was something he never forgot.

Daniel was kidnapped from his own country, probably as a teenager, and sent to Babylon. There he spent the rest of his life working for the king. In a foreign land with a fairly good job Daniel could have forgotten what he had been taught about God. He had a chance to start afresh and live how he wanted to live. However, from day one he told everyone who he was and what he stood for, refusing to compromise on his God.

It started with food and ended with lions. A typical Sunday-school story and yet a gripping drama of courage and trust. His witness of faith was so great that the king (his boss) said: 'May your God, whom you serve continually, rescue you' (Daniel 6:16).

Daniel's mates Shadrach, Meshach and Abednego were slung into a fiery furnace. They knew that without God they had no chance of surviving. In fact, they didn't know whether God would let them survive, but they stood up to the authorities and said: 'The God we serve is able to save us from [the blazing furnace], and he will rescue us from your hand, O king. But even if he does not, we want you to know, O king, that we will not serve your gods or worship the image of gold you have set up' (Daniel 3:17–18).

There's another Old Testament example where it didn't work out quite so well. In Genesis 39 we read how Joseph was hounded by the boss's wife and when he refused to sleep with her he was accused of rape and slung into jail. Now we know the end of the story, but at the time Joseph didn't. He was alone, in a dirty jail far away from home. He had little chance of getting out and it was all because he'd stuck by his principles and value-system. Yet, in time God used him to prevent famine in the land and blessed him with family, friends, power and wealth (Genesis 40 – 47).

Living in this world but having a value-system not of this world is not easy. In my office I am the only person who doesn't swear. People might notice I don't swear but they still swear around me. I've read books and heard sermons saying that if you don't swear, people won't swear around you and your influence can make your office a more righteous place. For me this hasn't been the case, but God still uses me in my office. Decide your own value-system, stick to it and people will notice even if they don't treat you differently because of it. Rob Parsons in his book *The Heart of Success* urges people not just to strive for success but to strive for significance. Your value-system can make a significant difference in your workplace.

In brief

God calls us to work.
Ask God for significance in what you do.
Know who you are and why you're doing that particular job.
Write a vision statement for your job.
How you do your work can make more of a difference than what you do.
Live with integrity.
Work can be your mission-field, look for God-opportunities there.

Further reading
The book of Daniel; look at how Daniel coped under pressure.
Mark Greene, *Thank God it's Monday: Ministry in the workplace* (Scripture Union, 1997).
Rob Parsons, *The Heart of Success* (Hodder and Stoughton, 2002).

chapter 5

workplace issues

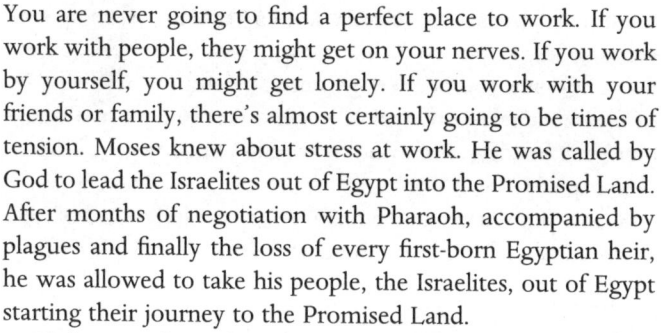

You are never going to find a perfect place to work. If you work with people, they might get on your nerves. If you work by yourself, you might get lonely. If you work with your friends or family, there's almost certainly going to be times of tension. Moses knew about stress at work. He was called by God to lead the Israelites out of Egypt into the Promised Land. After months of negotiation with Pharaoh, accompanied by plagues and finally the loss of every first-born Egyptian heir, he was allowed to take his people, the Israelites, out of Egypt starting their journey to the Promised Land.

Unfortunately, it didn't get any easier for Moses once he had left Egypt. The people demanded water, food, and then more interesting food. They made an idol of a golden calf, forsaking the Lord God who had brought them out of Egypt (Exodus 32). Moses had to cry out to God again and again asking for forgiveness for the Israelites. Even when work is really getting on your nerves, don't forget to pray for those you work with and for the work you do; things changed when Moses interceded.

real life | workplace issues

Time management
There are lots of great things about not being in full-time education anymore, and top of the list is money. However, two big drawbacks are the shorter holidays and inflexible working arrangements. Unlike university or college where you can manage your time how you want to, as long as you get through your work, a job usually involves set hours. This lack of flexibility can often bring extra stress as you try to juggle other commitments and expectations.

Every summer I consider going into teaching, tempted by the long holidays – until September when the schools go back and teachers start once again with a new list of names to memorize, children to control and every evening taken up with creating lesson plans and marking books. Most jobs (except teaching) give you between twenty-one and twenty-five days of paid holiday a year, which works out at four or five weeks plus bank holidays. It may not seem a lot, but you get used to it pretty quickly.

Good time-management can be particularly hard if you work shifts. Getting into a regular routine of eating properly,

---

Lack of personal time can become a major source of stress. Here are some tips on how to stop that happening and how to cope:
- Learn to be realistic about what you can and can't do. Don't plan to be away six weekends in a row. Going away every Friday night and coming back late every Sunday night leaves you no time to do your washing, go shopping and see those you live with. Enjoy your time off but make sure you are in a fit state to go to work on Monday morning.

- Does the company you work for have any flexible working arrangements? If you work extra hours, are you entitled to take them in lieu? Could you work four ten-hour days instead of the usual nine to five? Flexible working is a good way to accumulate extra holiday when your yearly quota is running a bit low.
- If you are working full-time, don't also work full-time for the church. It's healthy to serve your community and have interests outside work but you can't do forty hours a week on each. Ask God to use you where you are at work; this is a mission-field too.
- Consider working part-time. Ask yourself whether you need to work full-time: do you really need the money? Would working part-time significantly improve your quality of life? The problem with the rat race is that if you win you're still a rat!
- Spread your holiday throughout the year, don't take it all in March convinced you'll have left the company by July. It's always better to have a few days in hand just in case you win that free trip to Barbados!

reading the Bible and praying can seem almost impossible when it changes every week. The best way to make sure it all happens is to schedule in time for it. If you can't have a quiet time at the beginning of your day, decide when you can spend some time with God and keep to it. Do the same for eating, having time off and socializing. We all need balance in our lives.

Have a home–work balance

One of the things I love about Jesus is that when he was on earth he wasn't superhuman. He got tired, he cried, he needed time for himself and time to talk to God, and although it doesn't say it in the Bible, I'm sure he also needed the toilet. On one occasion, Jesus had just finished feeding 5,000 men and was tired. He could have done a number of things next; many people would have wanted to talk to him, invite him over for dinner, or maybe he could have healed a few more people? But he didn't do any of those things. Instead he went into the hills to pray (Mark 6:46). Jesus sent his disciples off in the opposite direction, dismissed the crowd and sought time for himself and God.

One of the best ways of practising good time-management is to learn to say 'no'. After the incident described above I'm sure Jesus had invitations to do other things, but he chose to get some space, clear his head and spend time with God. If you spend all your time at work, your relationship with God and with your friends is going to be affected. In a new job it can be hard to strike the right balance but even when you are trying to impress your employer, make sure your work doesn't take over your whole life.

My first experience of work was an industrial placement during my third year at university. I was part of a team of four. The rest of the team had worked together for many years and there was no-one who I was particularly good friends with, so I felt a strong pressure to conform and get along with them. The hours we worked were officially 10am till 6pm; the only problem was that at 6pm no-one wanted to go home. As the lowest person in the team and indeed the office I didn't want to look like I was uncommitted, so I'd stay for a bit until other people looked like they too were getting ready to leave. It would soon be twenty or thirty minutes or even an hour after the time I wished to go home.

At times there were immense amounts of work to do and we all had to stay late, but there were many times when I tried to look busy, too exhausted to do any more work, pretending to work and wishing I was at home. Having to look busy and working extra hours when you don't want to are two things that can make you feel depressed and worthless in the workplace.

It is often insecurity that forces people to work late. Your manager may feel insecure in his or her job and so stays late to look impressive; you then feel insecure at being the first to leave the office and so stay late too. It soon forms a negative cycle. Trying to conform to the negative aspects of an office culture can be soul-destroying but almost impossible not to do. Companies often recruit graduates from outside the area who have no social life, no friends and are happy to work long hours for something to do.

I once worked for a company whose management would regularly come in half-way through the afternoon and at 6pm call a meeting to discuss progress. The meeting would last at least one hour if not two. I was the only junior employee who had lived locally for more than six months, everyone else had come to the city specifically to work on that project and that's why the management got away with it.

The Financial Times comments on a report by the Institute of Management on Britain's long hours culture: 'The results underline a business case for reducing working hours. Stress and burn-out may be brushed aside as "personal problems" but the inefficient use of working hours must be a central concern for any business.'[1]

Working excessive hours produces poor workers. God calls us to work as though we were working for him not for people. He wants us to work well, but he wants us to work responsibly.

[1] Quoted in Rob Parsons, *The Heart of Success* (Hodder and Stoughton, 2002), p. 28.

We need to keep to the commitments we have made, keep up with our relationships and look after our own health. You matter to God, so behave like it!

I have a friend who is currently working in a temporary job that she doesn't particularly enjoy but has been doing for quite a while. Following a management restructure she now does the job of two people, leaving the house at 6.30am and returning often at 7.30pm or later. She finds it stressful, but says the work needs to be done. It does, but her managers need to realize it takes two people to do her job not one. If they don't listen, she needs to look for a new job.

There will always be situations where you need to stay late, and there is nothing wrong with that, but when you regularly face a situation where you can't finish your work in the set time or you feel unable to leave – something needs to change.

So what can you do about a workplace culture of long hours? There isn't an easy solution. You need to know who you are in God, and have the self-confidence to stand up for yourself and leave when you feel you should be leaving, refusing to conform to that kind of culture. If your work-mates around you are feeling the same way, send a joint memo to your manager or your manager's manager, explaining why you will be leaving at a particular time and why the work can't be finished in those hours.

If you work in a situation where you have responsibility to stay until someone else physically turns up, it may not be possible to insist on leaving at a certain time. However, it is still worth telling or writing to those in authority to explain the problems you are having and to try to reach an agreement for overtime pay. If people have to start paying you, their own time-management might get better. If you are part of a union, it might get involved and be able to negotiate on your behalf.

Most importantly, pray with Christian friends or colleagues in the same situation and ask their advice.

What did I do? None of the above. I left the company and promised myself I wouldn't get caught up in the same way in my next job. Thankfully, I had somewhere else to go. It was an easy way out and I didn't help anyone else by standing up to the culture or changing it from inside. I was too worried about what the management might think of me.

When I first started in my current job, leaving on time was something I found very hard to do. We work different shifts and this has the advantage of always having someone to hand unresolved work onto, and the disadvantage of people always staying later than you. It can be tempting to feel that you should stay too.

I am very committed to my job and if there was a genuine crisis I would come in from home or stay late. However, on a day-to-day basis to fulfil my commitments at home, at church, to co-run a youth group, to see my husband and friends, to meet up with the girls I mentor, to keep my house clean and hold on to my sanity I need to leave work on time!

As well as restricting your hours, to have a good work–home balance you need to leave your job at work. I know someone who on the way home metaphorically leaves her problems at a particular underground stop and refuses to think about them until the next day when she comes back into work. This can be hard when you are juggling so many different tasks and are worried what you might forget, but it is worth persevering with.

One thing I find helpful is to write a list of everything I need to do the next day when I leave work. Then when I get to work the next day I'm set up with a list of priorities without losing sleep about it overnight. God promises to carry our burdens for us, so why not give your problems to God to deal with overnight? This not only involves God in your work but also gives you a good excuse to forget about them!

Working with people

Working life is all about getting on with people; 99.9% of jobs involve working with people at some level. Some people choose a particular job because they want to work with people; others choose a different kind of job because they prefer to work mainly by themselves. Whatever your job is like there will be times when you love those around you and other times when you would gladly exchange them for a tank of goldfish.

'I had been there almost nine months and it was approaching my twenty-first birthday. I'd prepared some party invitations and had given them to a couple of friends at work. A few of the lads from the canteen had promised to come but my more immediate colleagues were all busy. I wasn't disappointed. It was hard work being a Christian in the office – whatever I did or said was always taken the wrong way.

'My birthday was at the weekend but my colleagues suggested going out for lunch on the Friday. It got to the end of the meal and they refused to let me pay. Then out of nowhere came a brightly wrapped present. Inside was a purse with twenty-one £1 coins in it. I was so surprised – I didn't even know they liked me.'

Those around you may not behave well. Your manager may be negative, spiteful and vindictive, but it doesn't mean that you have to follow suit. In the Bible the disciples argued about which of them was the greatest and who would sit next to Jesus in heaven. Jesus took a small child and told them that whoever wanted to be the greatest should be the least (Matthew 18:1–4).

'What really surprised me about work was that the simple things, like being well organized, nice to people, thoughtful and committed were what people appreciated. It didn't matter that I didn't necessarily know everything at the beginning.'

Often problems at work are the result of power dynamics. Jesus had the same issue with his disciples. Finding him on his own away from the other disciples, James and John asked Jesus for a favour: 'Let one of us sit at your right side and the other at your left in your glory' (Mark 10:37). What they were asking for was to be honoured as the second and third most important people in Jesus' kingdom. When the other disciples found out about this they were furious; maybe they were worried that they would be in twelfth place having not got in the queuing system early enough. Jesus, however, wasn't going to join in their political games of power. Instead he said: 'Whoever wants to become great among you must be your servant, and whoever wants to be first must be slave of all' (Mark 10:43–44).

Don't be afraid to serve those on your team and those around you. Little things can make a real difference and improve the whole atmosphere of your office. Why not bring in some cookies and offer to make everyone coffee? Or organize a get-well card when someone is ill? Try to accept people the way they are and ask God for help in improving your relationship with them.

If you don't know something, ask. People would usually prefer to explain something that you don't understand rather than have you fail to finish the task because you weren't exactly sure what you were meant to be doing.

Temptation

Work is an obvious place for temptation. Often it is a place where people don't know your background, your faith, your real life | workplace issues

> ### *How to cope with temptation at work:*
> - Tell people you are a Christian, so that even if they don't believe what you believe, they might expect you to behave in a certain way and may not include you in risqué situations.
> - Don't engage in inappropriate relationships even when it just seems like a bit of fun.
> - Get an accountability partner who will ask you the questions you hate to answer.
> - Look out for possible support systems in your workplace. Are there other Christians you can pray with?
> - Be sensible and don't flirt with fire.

friends or partner. You may end up travelling alone on business trips, where there is no accountability. No-one knows what you are watching in your hotel room. No-one knows what clubs you may visit or what expenses are really legitimate. Often it comes down to you, your conscience and God.

'I travel a lot away from home for work, so to avoid watching pornography on the TV I bring my Playstation. I'm now getting quite good.'

When talking about temptation, the Bible tells us to flee from it not flirt with it. On a practical level this means helping yourself by not seeing how close you can get to the fire without getting burnt. King David played with fire in 2 Samuel 11. In the spring when kings usually went to war David was at home with nothing to do. Bored, he started spying on a woman bathing. He then slept with her and she fell pregnant.

David invited her husband Uriah home from the war, hoping he would sleep with his wife and no-one would know the baby was David's. It didn't work and so David had Uriah killed to hide his own sin. If David hadn't started watching Bathsheba bathing, and then fantasized about her, none of it would have happened.

When you are tempted, distract yourself. Phone a friend for an accountability chat, go to the cinema, or find the local leisure centre and do a vigorous workout. If your company has sent you away from home for a number of weeks, why not consider getting involved in a local church? They might have a midweek meeting you could go to.

In brief

Manage your time outside work in a way that doesn't compromise your time in work.
Investigate flexible working.
Have a home–work balance.
Serve those around you.
Be wise and be aware of temptations at work.
Set up support systems to deal with those temptations.

Further reading
Rob Parsons, *The Heart of Success* (Hodder and Stoughton, 2002).

63

chapter 6

a new place

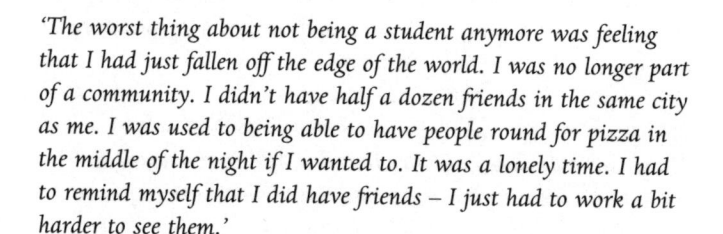

'The worst thing about not being a student anymore was feeling that I had just fallen off the edge of the world. I was no longer part of a community. I didn't have half a dozen friends in the same city as me. I was used to being able to have people round for pizza in the middle of the night if I wanted to. It was a lonely time. I had to remind myself that I did have friends – I just had to work a bit harder to see them.'

Starting again in a new place can be really hard. If you're lucky, a group of you will be going to the same place and you can share a house and have a great time with hopefully a little more money than when you were students. But for most people leaving university is a new start where they have to make new friends and find a new church as well as get settled into their new job.

In the Bible, Abram (soon to be called Abraham) was a man called by God to move to a new place and start again. God tells Abram: 'Leave your country, your people and your father's household and go to the land I will show you' (Genesis 12:1). Abram was told to leave all he knew; he had no children and was leaving his family who would have cared

real life | a new place

for him in old age. It was an uncertain time, but Abram obeyed God. He took his wife and nephew and settled in Canaan. In this new land Abram could have felt sorry for himself far away from those he knew. As head of his now very small household he had no-one to be accountable to and could have indulged in wild parties and forgotten about God. But he didn't; he still listened to God, God spoke to him and Abram built a public altar as an acknowledgment of the relationship between them.

Starting again in a new place may not be easy but make sure you carry on talking and listening to God. Like Abram, be public about your worship, make a conscious decision to worship God both on your own and within a community of other Christians.

'It was my first Sunday and I was desperate to find some Christians and make some friends. It had been a lonely few days not knowing anyone and although I didn't want to be cliquey and only hang out with Christians I didn't know anyone else and church is a place where you can talk to people without them getting the wrong idea about you. Besides it was my only chance of getting a free Sunday lunch!

'I was only 15 minutes early but as with most church services 15 minutes early might as well be three days. I was greeted at the door by a lovely old lady who said something about it being nice to see young people in the church. Alarm bells started to ring but I smiled a nice holy Christian smile and allowed her to show me where to sit.

'The church service came and went. I can remember nothing about it, apart from being introduced to a thirty-something father because he was a "young person" and being told about a communal church lunch in three weeks' time. I left more lonely and fed up than when I walked through the door.'

Moving to a new place is often hard, especially if you work anti-social hours and weekends or if you have the kind of job where you will spend three months in one place before moving on. Finding friends and a church family can be crucial in making a place home.

Get plugged into a church

When my husband Tim graduated, he moved to London and spent the first three months looking for a church. It's hard when the only meetings are on Sundays and your girlfriend lives in another city. The problem with London is that it's all so big. People commute so far to go to work, and they often do the same for church. This can make it hard to develop friendships.

Looking for churches in London we went to all the big names and several small ones chosen at random. Eventually we ended up at a fantastic church where there was a community of people who loved each other, loved God and loved those around them. It became a home not only for Tim but for me too on my frequent visits to the capital.

When moving to a new city don't spend three months church-shopping and making yourself miserable. Ask friends and family, people you trust. Get a recommendation, stick with it and get plugged in. If you dither around for three months you may not want to go anywhere at the end of it.

One of the most powerful sermons I have remembered from my teenage years was a youth pastor saying, 'Is church nothing more than a social club or dating agency, or is it a body of believers prepared to get its hands dirty and partake in the world's pain?' Your church may not be perfect, but in a strange place you need a church to help and encourage you to be an effective witness for Christ. They need you too. Don't let your church become your social circle, but let it real life | a new place

sustain your social circle so you can reach out to those around you.

Stick with it, live in it

'Life after university can be tough and it is easier if you are expecting it to be like that. Decide to be proactive in seeking out friendships. You'll soon get used to turning up at meetings and events knowing no-one. It gets easier once you introduce yourself to people. Taking up an evening class or gym class can be a great way of getting to know new people.'

It may be hard, but sticking in a place for as long as possible can really help you get plugged in. If you go away every weekend to visit friends, it will be very hard to settle in the town or city where you work. One of the easiest things to do after you have left full-time education is to remember the past and not live in the present. It may have been hard work, with stressful deadlines and friendship bust-ups, but too often we remember the sunshine and none of the reality.

The Israelites did the same thing. In Egypt they moaned and groaned, asking God to deliver them from their labour, asking for their own land and freedom. Yet in the desert they said to Moses: 'Was it because there were no graves in Egypt that you brought us to the desert to die? What have you done to us by bringing us out of Egypt?' (Exodus 14:11).

Let God use the time and the place you are in now to help shape you into the person he wants you to be. Loneliness breeds self-pity and bad habits. Whatever your particular problem area is, whether it is food or bad telly, don't let it get control of your life now. Don't let loneliness get the upper hand. Resist the urge to spend all your free time visiting old friends around the country, instead, get out and meet new people, make new friends. Really live where you are staying. As well as getting stuck into a church, get involved in other activities too. Going swimming at the same time every week may help you to build up friendships with other people who go at the same time. Or join a special interest group. Get to know your neighbours – it's amazing how many people you can find to say hello to when you water a plantpot outside your house every evening!

Moving to a new place is hard and being taken out of your comfort zone can make you either regress or grow up. Life in the new land of Canaan wasn't easy for Abram. Soon there was a famine and he had to leave the place God had called him to and move on to Egypt, a place where he feared for his life because of his wife's beauty (Genesis 12:10–20). However, through all the difficult times Abram carried on talking to God and walking with him. Returning to the desert after being evicted by the Egyptians God continued to speak to him and promised him his one heart-felt desire, a son.

I love the poem quoted on page 6 of this book, especially these lines:

> I said to the man
> Who stood at the gate of the year
> 'Give me a light that I may tread safely
> into the unknown.'
> And he replied,
> 'Go into the darkness
> and put your hand into the hand of God
> That shall be to you
> Better than light
> And safer than a known way!'

That's what we need to do; put our hand in God's and ask him to show us the way. He has promised he will always be there with us; when it's tough and when it's easy.

Keep in touch and encourage each other
In the third year of my course I spent a year in industry which meant I moved down to Bristol while everyone else stayed in Leeds. All of my friends were useless at keeping in touch except for two who were doing similar placements. After university ended and we were scattered all over the country, I noticed people suddenly got a lot better!

Whether it is you that needs the support, or one of your mates that is going through a hard time, keeping in touch with friends really helps. An unexpected letter or random phone call can make someone's day. Listen and support people without it becoming a moaning session. Try to end each phone call by praying together.

Know where you've come from and where you're going
Finally, get out that list you made in your final year (or make one now) and remind yourself of who you are. What are the skills and abilities God has given you? What specific words of encouragement have people said about you? Whether it was a 'holy moment' or not it doesn't matter, find out who you are in God. Look for God's perspective on where you are now and the struggles you are facing. Are you letting God use your situation to develop your character?

In brief

a new place

Get plugged into a church quickly, don't spend months finding the perfect one.

Let your church sustain your social circle not be your social circle; make other friends too!

Like Abram, stick with it. Ask God for his help.

Don't live in a world of memories. Keep in touch with good friends and encourage each other.

Remind yourself why you're there.

Let God use the tough times to make you more like him.

Further reading
Read Joshua 1 and 2. Look at how God spoke to the Israelites when they were moving to a new land.

chapter 7

money!

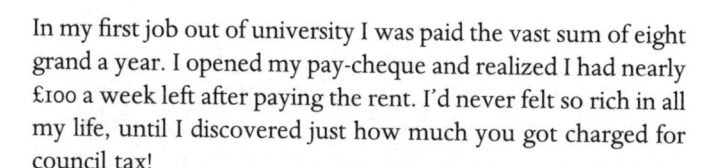

In my first job out of university I was paid the vast sum of eight grand a year. I opened my pay-cheque and realized I had nearly £100 a week left after paying the rent. I'd never felt so rich in all my life, until I discovered just how much you got charged for council tax!

There are lots of books about money, how to use money: how not to use money and so on. For most ex-students their first job post-education is a time when suddenly they have some spare cash – often not much cash, but usually some. Deciding how to spend it, save it and give it in the first few weeks can set a precedent for the rest of your life.

Money is worthless when you die

Remember in the film *Titanic* where Caledon Hockley tries to buy his way onto a lifeboat? First Officer Mr Murdock tells him, 'Your money can't save you anymore than it can save me.' The one thing that has given him security all his life is suddenly worthless; you can't buy your way off a sinking boat. Again and again in the Bible God reminds us of this principle. In the Old Testament God says, 'Neither their silver nor their gold will be able to save them on the day of the LORD's wrath'

(Zephaniah 1:18). We can't buy God's favour with our money. Jesus told many stories about money. One was about a man who stored up treasures in a barn and then died before he could spend it (Luke 12:16–21). It is important to save money and use money responsibly but not to be obsessed with the things of this world where fashions change with the wind and where thieves break in and steal our possessions. As Jesus said, 'Where your treasure is, there your heart will be also' (Matthew 6:21).

God calls us to be good stewards of all we have and reminds us many times that all we have comes from him. Psalm 24:1 says: 'The earth is the LORD's and everything in it, the world, and all who live in it.' However much we have, whether we feel rich or poor, it all belongs to God and he has generously shared it with us. We need to keep this in mind when we spend what we consider 'our' money. God doesn't tell us that if we give away 10% we are doing well and then we can spend the rest on what we want, instead he says we can serve either him or money (Matthew 6:24). It is a choice.

How much should you give away?

'As soon as we have some excess money we drift so easily into a culture of ever-increasing accumulation. John Wesley figured out how much he needed to live on and then gave the rest away. At first he gave a little away, but by the end of his ministry he was giving away a lot. We get trapped into a culture of needing more and more. Before you have a lot of money learn to live below your means, spend some money, save some and give some away.'

So often we give on a whim. Whether it is to the homeless person on the street or the visiting preacher who has a wife and three kids, we give casually out of our excess without it really hurting our pockets.

In the Old Testament God calls the Israelites to give of the first-fruits of their harvest, that is the bit at the beginning, not the bit at the end. I've recently taken up vegetable gardening and at the moment my broad beans are just starting to produce pods. Remembering how much I hated them being tough and stringy as a child, last night I picked them. My first-fruits amounted to about eight pods, producing in total about two tablespoons of broad beans, not much considering how long it took me to water them!

Now on those plants I can't see many new pods developing. If those beans were all I had to live on I would need a lot of faith to give those first new ones to God. What happens if a plague of blackfly descends or snails eat the new shoots? What if we have a drought or the next-door neighbour's cat decides to dig them up? Where will the rest of my crop be then?

Giving to God is never easy, but the Israelites who God gave this command to were peasant farmers surviving on a few acres of land; it must have been a lot harder for them. All our money is God's and we should listen to him about what to give away.

Making regular donations by standing order or direct debit is an important way to give to your church or chosen charity. It means you're giving out of the first-fruits of your wages, not whatever is left in your pocket after a Saturday night out. Another advantage is that charities can claim back the tax, increasing your donation by 30%.

What if you don't have enough money?

'The house was dusty and small. To keep the fridge shut you needed to lean an ironing board against the door. The freezer shelf had been broken by the sheer volume of water which formed solid ice at the top of the fridge and dripped continuously onto the food below.

'It was an unusual arrangement, two twenty-somethings and one old lady in her seventies, but there was little else you could get for £63 per week in central London. The place I'd lived in before was damp and cold and at least this house had central heating!

'There were three of us in the house: myself, who earned £8,000 a year, not much for such an expensive capital; a sheltered graduate who had stacks of money from Daddy and no common sense; and a lonely old lady who wanted some company. It was a curious mix, but I was grateful. I couldn't have afforded anything else!'

For some people trying to raise their own finances for a voluntary project or those who aren't earning enough to cover their rent and bills graduating can seem very tough. Suddenly all your friends are organizing expensive trips away, throwing stag and hen weekends that may cost several hundred pounds, and you feel like you can't keep up.

If you don't have the money, don't let people think you have. It quickly becomes a dangerous cycle, and there's nothing wrong with saying 'Sorry I can't afford that this month.' Many ex-students have a lot of debt already, so don't get drawn into more debt by credit cards that promise easy terms and low-interest payments. Throw the flyers away before you are tempted.

Sometimes starting a new job means you have to borrow money to buy a car or put down a large deposit for accommodation. But where possible try to save up for things rather than take out loans – that way *you* get to keep the interest not the bank. If you do have to take out a loan ask other people for advice and look carefully at the level of interest you have to pay. It may be cheaper to get a loan from your bank to buy a car rather than taking up the finance deal offered by the garage.

'I graduated in July and we got married in August. It was very tough financially at first. I was working but my wife had two years left as a student. I needed a car for work and if it had gone wrong we had no money to pay for a replacement. We were really strict about what we could spend on ourselves and had £5 each a week and that was it. We saved a few pounds every month in case there were problems with the car, and sure enough by the end of the year it needed replacing! I don't know what we would have done if we hadn't been so careful with our money.'

Don't forget the little things you can do to make a difference yourself. Take a bottle of water to work with you so you don't have to buy a drink out. Make your sandwiches the night before instead of buying them. Three pounds five times a week quickly adds up to £15, that's nearly £800 over a year – enough for a luxury holiday.

Budgeting

Once you start spending money it can be very hard to stop. It's a lot easier not to spend it in the first place, and one way to do this is to budget. Budgeting is a way of exercising discipline on how you spend your money, by choosing to set limitations on how much you spend on particular things. This takes into account fixed expenditure, such as rent, flexible but necessary expenditure, like food, and chosen expenditure, like leisure activities. Knowing how much money you need to live on and how much you are choosing to spend can help you get a good perspective on how much to give away.

By writing down a budget and sticking to it you can assess at the end of the month whether you are spending your money according to your priorities, and if not you can see where it is going. If you have set an unrealistic budget you can

How to set a budget

- Write down all your fixed outgoings: rent, bills, loans, travel expenses.
- Look through your bank statements and see how much money you are spending on flexible essentials such as food or phone bills. Ask your friends and family how much they spend and set yourself a target amount that you don't want to exceed. (This will require you to know approximately how much you are spending on these items throughout the month so that you don't exceed the limit.) Be realistic about what you are going to spend – are you prepared not to make any phone calls if you exceed your limit, or live on baked beans for a week if you spend your month's allowance on takeaways?
- Finally, look at what you have left and decide how much you are going to give away, save, spend on leisure, the gym, weekends away, clothes, etc. Do allow yourself to go out and remember some months will be more expensive than others. Christmas may cost you a lot, but maybe you spent almost nothing in August as all your expenditure came out of your holiday budget not your social budget. Creative budgeting can be great fun!
- Once you have decided how much you want to spend on everything try to keep to it. Pay for items by Switch and keep your receipts so it is easy to see what you are spending where. Then at the end of each month check how your budget is going and re-evaluate your expenditure.

adjust it accordingly; if you need to be more self-disciplined you know which weaknesses you need to address.

If your budgeting falls flat on its face the first time you do it, don't despair – assess where you went wrong and what you might need to change, then try again. Even if you spend more than your budget may allow, you will probably still have spent less than if you had no budget at all. Assess your budget monthly (at least) and if you're really struggling take it to someone you trust and ask for their help.

Don't attempt to write down every single newspaper and can of coke – allow yourself to spend a certain amount of untraceable cash every week on those non-essentials. You can budget on paper, spreadsheets, palm tops, whatever is most helpful. Remember, a budget is there to make your life easier, but it might take a bit of practice to get it right!

Manage your bank account
Even if you don't set budgets, to keep out of the red you'll need to make sure you know what is in your bank account, so check your balance before you get money out. Organize your account, especially your giving and saving, so you don't have a lot of excess money in your current account just begging to be spent.

One good way to do this is to set up standing orders from your current account and have a savings account that requires a cheque book or a trip to the bank if you want extra money. If your savings aren't as accessible as your current account, it may mean you think twice about whether you really want to spend the money.

Temptations
All possessions cost time, money and effort to buy them and maintain them. Labour-saving devices give us more time to be

busier, while barbecues and fondue sets give us more stuff to store, dust and clean. In the West we are always tempted to spend money on things we don't need, whether it is clothes, CDs or music equipment. It's good to know what you have a weakness for so you can watch out for it and check your spending is righteous and not out of control.

My big temptation is DIY. As soon as we bought a house I found a whole new area of spending that I could justify and that was socially acceptable. I was no longer participating in mass consumerism, instead I was 'investing' in my house. If we buy a new fireplace, maybe the property's value will go up. If we install a fountain in the garden, it might make the house more sellable. It all sounds very rational and thought out, but the underlying root was 'I want it and I want it now!' Luxuries are quickly renamed as necessities.

God has no problem with me having a nice house and garden, but he does have a problem with millions of his children starving to death. God doesn't expect me to go and join them and starve myself in sympathy, but he does expect me to live a life of social responsibility to others in this world. Let us not be like the rich fool in Jesus' story, so busy hoarding our money or possessions that we lose perspective on the world around us (Luke 12:16–21).

Life not image

You're walking along the street on a night out. You've got £20 in your pocket which will just about cover your entry fee to the club, a few drinks and a taxi home. A homeless man asks you for a few pence change. You saw him earlier that day and didn't give him anything but he now looks more desperate and your mates are watching. What do you do?

Who we are with so often affects what we do. God calls us to be the same whoever we are with. He is always watching us! Don't give money so you look good in front of your mates, give out of the goodness God has given to you.

I recently read a travel review of a holiday in a South African game park. (I've always wondered who actually pays for these trips – I wouldn't mind reviewing a holiday or two!) In the middle of the article there was one small paragraph describing how to get to the game park the journalist had driven through several of South Africa's townships and the people were very poor and it was all very sad. Then in the next sentence she was back in the full flow of her lovely holiday story. Throughout the Bible God calls us to remember the poor consistently, not just occasionally when we want to look good in front of our mates or randomly in a fit of guilt, when we feel the need to atone for our middle-class lifestyle. God calls us to find his heart of justice for those who are struggling.

In Luke, Jesus rebukes the teachers of the day saying: 'Woe to you Pharisees, because you give God a tenth of your mint, rue and all other kinds of garden herbs, but you neglect justice and the love of God. You should have practised the latter without leaving the former undone' (Luke 11:42). Do we practise justice when we spend our money? Do we buy products that have exploited those who have made them, or do we try to buy fair-trade products and invest in companies that have an ethical investment policy? Jesus wasn't saying it was wrong to tithe mint and ruc but he was saying that the Pharisees needed to live out their whole life in line with the gospel. It may cost more to buy fair-trade coffee but we need to involve God in how we spend all our money, not just our 'tithe'.

Accountability

Consider showing your bank statement to a friend. Letting someone else see where you spend your money can really make you think: it can be hard trying to explain to an independent witness why you needed a fourth pair of trainers that month. Alternatively they might tell you that you are being too hard on yourself and since you're exhausted you should spend some money on a retreat or luxury holiday. Having to get your books in order for someone else is a fantastic way of forcing yourself to work out where all your money is going.

Not just money
So often we talk about tithing or giving money without also giving sacrificially of our time. If we give God money from our earnings but otherwise ignore his involvement in the rest of our lives, we are letting him partake in only 50% of our lives. Don't forget to invest your time in God's kingdom as well, remembering that where your treasure is, your heart is also (Matthew 6:21).

I was recently discussing 'grace' with some friends. It's an outrageous concept. Jesus' message was that people don't get what they deserve but are given unconditional acceptance and love. We were talking about accepting people regardless of what they do and befriending them. These may be people we like but can often be people we find difficult to hang out with. Yet in these relationships God uses them to challenge us. If we only hang around with people we like, or those who we would naturally associate with, we isolate ourselves from God. We no longer need his help in our relationships and can forget he is there until a 'designated church time' or 'quiet time'.

When you leave education you will be busy, life will be pressured. Houses need to be cleaned and clothes washed, but take time to ask God what he wants you to do with your life. You may feel like you have no time now, but commitments have a way of building up – in twenty years time you may be caring for elderly relatives or running round after three kids and a dog!

In brief

All of your money is from God in the first place.
Give of your first-fruits, set up standing orders to give money away before you have spent it.
Give consistently.
Look after your bank account.
Set yourself budgets, try to keep to them or failing that look at why you are not keeping to them.
Throw away credit-card adverts.
Consider talking to a friend about what you spend your disposable income on.
Know your temptations.
Giving is a lifestyle not an image.
Giving is more than just money.

Further reading
Ronald J. Sider, *Rich Christians in an Age of Hunger* (Hodder, 1990).
Philip Yancey, *What's so Amazing about Grace?* (Zondervan, 1997).
Christopher D. Hudson, et al., *Money: Clues for the Clueless* (Barbour & Co., 2000).

chapter 8

gap years

It's not what you do it's how you do it
Gap years can be a great opportunity to have a break before you start working life while gaining some vital qualifications and life skills, or they can be a great delaying tactic, fending off the day you have to settle down to the scary world of work.

In the Bible Jesus tells a story about a prodigal son (Luke 15:11–32). He is using the story to illustrate God's relationship with us, but it can also shed some light on important lessons about gap years and other short-term projects. It deals with three areas that are particularly relevant to gap years: money, relationships and keeping your focus.

In the story a son goes to his father and asks for his inheritance. Now this wasn't money he had earned, it was what he would inherit when his father died. Because his father loved him he gave him the money. His son promptly left home and spent it all on 'wild living'. A few years later he has lost everything and has been reduced to feeding pigs in a faraway land. He decides to go home, realizing that even his father's servants are fed better than he is. The father welcomes him home and celebrates his return saying, 'This son of mine was dead and is alive again; he was lost but now he is found' (Luke 15:24).

real life | gap years

The first lesson we can learn from this story is to do with money. The son effectively borrowed money to start his new life. When he returned to his father's house he had nothing, having spent his inheritance, leaving no provision for his future. There may be many reasons why you want to take a gap year now, but if you are intending to borrow money for it, work out a plan for paying it back. Can you organize a job now for when you return? Debts have a nasty habit of hanging over you and interest can mount up, especially if it takes you a while to find a job when you return.

The second unwise thing the son did was to neglect all his relationships. His father didn't know where his son was; although he kept looking out for him, he feared his son was dead. While his father welcomed him back with open arms, his older brother couldn't accept the situation quite so easily and was angry at all the fuss that was being made. When you return from your gap year it's important to recognize that relationships will be different. Your siblings may be jealous of adventures you may have had while they have stayed at home. In breaking off all his relationships with his family and friends the son didn't have anyone asking him difficult questions and holding him accountable. Whether you are doing a specifically Christian project in your gap year or just travelling with some friends, make sure you keep in contact with people who will support you in your Christian life and hold you accountable for what you do. Don't neglect important relationships.

Thirdly, the son lost his vision. He had spent all his money and had no idea what to do. Hungry, he took a job feeding the pigs, a job that made him ritually unclean according to Jewish law. Make sure you have purpose in your gap year. Assess what are you trying to do. It might be a spiritual or physical goal, but make sure you have a goal and set yourself targets to achieve it. A gap year is only a limited period of time, make sure you use it well.

When the son came to his senses, he returned home and begged the forgiveness of his father. This is the great climax of the story. The son was welcomed home and reinstated in the household. He took responsibility for what he had done and apologized to his father, but this isn't the end of the story. His older brother was angry, and refused to come inside and join in the feast. Things may seem difficult when you come back from your gap year, especially if you are returning to a boring job or a difficult living arrangement – keeping up relationships while you are away may help with this. Be prepared to serve those around you and work on neglected relationships.

There is nothing wrong with taking a gap year and many employers value the experience gained in them, but make sure you carry on moving forward in your gap year and use the time to broaden your life experience.

'In the third year of my degree I made a vague arrangement to travel to the Middle East with some friends from university. I got a job for six months to save up some money, while living with my parents, and then went to Egypt, Jordan, Israel and Palestine. We spent three months working with a Palestinian NGO and through doing this I found out what I wanted to do with my life. I decided I wanted to work in campaigning and not journalism as I had previously thought. I'm glad I went as it gave me a real chance to explore the gifts God has given me.'

Make a decision – don't drift
Gap years are great when planned carefully and when God is involved. What you need to avoid doing is drifting into a gap year because it is easier to organize than the real world of work.

'I felt awful at home with my parents after university. I had been so focused on my exams and degree that I had never thought past it. I was praying for destiny and found it easier to get on a mission ladder than career ladder. I missed the close community of student life, and mission was a very similar and comfortable environment to work in.'

Many ex-students have had great gap years which turn into full-time work in an area to which they feel God has called them, which is fantastic. However, some people use the year after university to hang around and put off the real decision of what to do in life.

'I was totally fed up with my degree and didn't want to get a job, I wanted to do something completely different with my life. I applied to work in a voluntary capacity for four charities and ended up working with homeless people on a farm in Yorkshire. God taught me a lot about hard work that year, I was the laziest slacker ever! I don't think I had ever done a hard day's work in my life before.

'It wasn't an easy environment to work in. I was told what to do all day everyday. I was at the bottom of the heap and no-one ever listened to me. After I finished there I still didn't know what to do, so I tried working in a care home. That was great because I found out that social work or care work wasn't for me. I re-assessed what I wanted to do with my life and decided maybe God wanted me to use my degree in maths. I then applied for anything and everything to do with maths and computers and now I really feel that's where God wants me to be.'

God uses gap years to teach us many different things. Ask God where he is leading you, what he is developing in you and what he wants you to do next.

It might not be easy
Some gap years can feel like a natural progression of life, but others can be much tougher. Being in a new place and trying to make new friends can feel like hard work rather than a chosen opportunity.

'My gap year was one of those experiences which looking back on you appreciate, but it wasn't easy at the time. But it was something I had wanted to do and I was glad that I had done it.'

Challenges never feel great at the time but can help us hear God more clearly. Don't be afraid of something new, and remember to look for God in the obstacles you face.

'I worked for a charity for a year when I graduated. Unfortunately, since they paid me peanuts, they didn't seem to value my time and often I was left to look busy with little if any work to do. At the time I didn't have enough confidence either to go home or to ask other people for more work.'

It has been said that people value you as much as they pay you. If you are working for free, don't let people abuse you and your time. Often people feel like they don't have time to explain how to do their job and operate on the principle 'It's easier to do it myself.' Show them where you can help out, be faithful in the work you do and be assertive in giving and asking for feedback.

It's never too late ...
Finally, it's never too late. Don't be afraid to get off the treadmill of work and do something different for a while. You may not have taken a gap year after school or university – why not do so now? Some jobs offer unpaid leave after you have

been there for a few years. In some careers it may be possible to get a new job quickly when you return.

'As a doctor I had just spent six months working in the accident and emergency department and had to escape. I was working two weekends a month and lots of late nights and shifts. I was only seeing my housemates and friends occasionally and decided I had had enough. I went to New Zealand for six months and chilled out. It gave me renewed enthusiasm for my job when I came back.'

God often teaches you a lot when you are away from all your home comforts and put into a new situation. Don't ignore the chance for him to shake up your life. It's never too late!

In brief

Don't delay the world of work by taking a gap year, take it and use it to become more like the person God has called you to be.
Don't expect it to be easy.
Be assertive, don't let people devalue you just because they don't pay you.
It's never too late to get off the treadmill of work, many employers let people take unpaid leave for a limited amount of time.

chapter 9

relationships

Jesus loved people: little people, big people, fat people, thin people. God made us all and he thinks we're all great. Paul tells us very clearly in 1 Corinthians that we are all part of one body, we all need each other and God has arranged the parts in the body as he wanted them to be (1 Corinthians 12:12–26). As people in your friendship group pair up, get engaged and then married, it can be easy to forget that God calls us to be one body. Sometimes we may look at other people and couples and wish we were more like them. But, Paul argues, if we all wanted to be an eye, where would the sense of hearing be? Or if we wanted to be an ear, where would the sense of smell be? We all have special gifts and abilities that are unique to us. As people pair off, it's important to remember that all of us are needed in the body of Christ.

People in full-time education are often in a more diverse state of boyfriend-girlfriend relationships than they are a few years after leaving. Long-distance relationships often lead to people splitting up or making the commitment to get married, and within five years it may seem as if all your Christian friends have fallen into one of the two camps.

For some people this can lead to them associating only with

people in a similar state to themselves. Couples may just invite other couples to dinner as they think a single person might feel awkward, while single people may choose not to hang around with couples as they assume they need time alone together. All communities work best with a mixture of people, as Paul agrees above, and through understanding the issues different people face in their relationships, we can make sure our friends stay our friends regardless of whether they are single or married.

Singleness in brief

We are all born single and all die alone. There may be many myths about finding your other half or of marriages made in heaven, but the Bible says nothing about this. God made us complete people. You don't have to get married to fulfil your destiny; singleness is not a transitory stage we go through until we get married.

Some people may feel that God has a specific job for them which they can do better single, and may therefore choose to remain single. Others might not meet a suitable marriage partner and so they too remain single. Some people may be happy in their single state, while others wish they had a partner.

Marriage in brief

Some people choose to get married after deciding they want to spend the rest of their life with a particular person. Through a public ceremony they make vows of commitment before their friends, family and God. For many people growing up in a culture where one in three marriages end in divorce, making the decision to marry may need a lot of faith both in God and in the other person.

Once you are married it doesn't mean you will live happily

ever after. Relationships take time to maintain. And then there's the matter of children. Once married, it can't automatically be assumed that a couple can have or that they even want them.

Neither being married nor being single makes you a better or more fulfilled person; but using the circumstances in which you live for God does.

Relationship confusion

We all need relationships
In Genesis God said: 'It is not good for the man to be alone ...' (Genesis 2:18), and he created Eve. God created someone for Adam to have fun with, someone to share stuff with, someone who was like him but different. We all need relationships; some people may get married, others never will. But while we may not all have partners, we all need friends. It is not good for us to live alone and God knew that, therefore he created families and communities.

One single person says:

'We all need each other and often people don't realize that. Married people need me to take the kids off their hands or to be a sane adult to talk to after they have been with toddlers all day. I need them too. I need hugs from kids and to have people around who care about me. I need to borrow men when I have a DIY problem round my house.'

Another married person agrees:

'I remember getting married and thinking how boring it would be to live with only one person after the rich variety of housemates I was used to. I love my spouse but often I need other company.'

> **Practical suggestions:**
> - Next time you have some friends round to dinner invite someone you haven't seen for a while and perhaps wouldn't naturally think to include.
> - Don't assume people are too busy to see you or would feel awkward – ask them and allow them to make up their own mind.

We need to live in relationship with people around us. Whether we're married, single, widowed, whether we have kids or not, every person needs people around them to support them. Whether our friends get married or remain single, it is important to remain in community with them. We may find their partner or children frustrating, or we may feel as if they don't understand us. Friends, like families, can be exasperating but we need to forgive and move on.

Is singleness a gift?

Some people may feel called to be single, others may not. But assuming that some people are given a supernatural gift of singleness while others are just wiling away the time until Mr or Mrs Right comes along means we can fail to support people or, more importantly, can fail to view singleness as a state to be lived in rather than a state to wait in. This assumption can also give married people an illusion of superiority, making them seem older and wiser and therefore more suitable for church leadership.

In 1 Corinthians 7 Paul talks about the gift of singleness. It has been argued that this is a spiritual gift and so the implication is that some people are given it and some aren't. This viewpoint can make single people feel under pressure to

> ***Practical suggestions:***
> - Encourage single friends to make the most of life in their single state, and not wait around for the right person before they can fulfil their lifelong calling.
> - If you're single, don't allow yourself to feel inferior or less of a person for not being in a couple. God has given you an equal gift, and will give you the community and support mechanisms you need.

discern whether or not they have the gift of singleness. Al Hsu in his book *The Single Issue* argues that it is not a spiritual gift, just a gift from God. In the same way, marriage is a God-given gift:

> ... the 'gift of singleness' is not something that must be spiritually discerned or subjectively felt. Singles do not need to search their hearts to see if they are truly able to live as contented singles. It is not some supernatural empowerment for some function of ministry. Rather, the gift is a description of an objective status. *If you are single, then you have the gift of singleness. If you are married, you don't.* If you marry, you exchange the gift of singleness for the gift of marriedness. Both are good.[1]

In changing our understanding of how we view singleness and marriage, as both equal gifts from God, we can help support each other better.

---

[1] Al Hsu, *The Single Issue* (Inter-Varsity Press, 1997), p. 61.

Wedded bliss?

I remember being told as a teenager that spending all your time day-dreaming about someone is emotional pornography and can be just as crippling as physical pornography. Don't do the same with marriage: wasting your life dreaming of wedded bliss instead of getting on with the business of living.

'The thing that has helped me be most content with being single is seeing married people at close quarters.'

It can be easy for people, especially women, to have a mental calendar in their head, planning to get married by *x* year so that they can have a family *y* years after, before they are *z* age. When things don't seem to be happening as planned, it can be easy to panic and look at married people with envy. But marriage isn't easy.

'Christian friends assumed that because I was getting married I was sorted. Actually it was pretty difficult. Friends at work made a lot of snide comments and some people thought I was getting married so that at long last I could have sex. I found it hard to explain coherently why I wanted to get married.'

Getting married doesn't guarantee that you will have children. Whether you want children and are married or unmarried the only thing you can do is take it to God and let him use you and your desires.

'I know that God has called me to be a father to those kids around where we live. I may not have kids but I can still make a difference in kids' lives on an estate where there are many single-parent families. I try to be a positive role model, taking kids to see a football match or helping them repair their bikes.'

> **Practical suggestions:**
> - Support married friends, reaffirm them in their relationships and the commitments they have made.
> - If you're single and want to be married don't be jealous from a distance of your married friends' relationships. Spend time with them, help out with their kids, use the gifts God has given you to bless others.
> - If you are married, make sure you schedule in time to see your partner. Don't get into the mould of hanging round with couples only, see your single friends too.

God calls us to live in community, and in sharing the highs and lows of our lives together we can share in both the pain and the joys.

Other issues involving relationships

The first university wedding
'It was the first university wedding I had been to and actually it really scared me. I had forgotten how serious a commitment marriage is. It's not just a party to celebrate when you can have sex, but it's a commitment in front of God for ever.'

Life can seem very weird when the first of your friends gets married. They may have been together for ages, but when the thousands of pounds get blown on that single day suddenly something changes and you may not be sure how to relate to them any more. Everyone is different, but at the end of the day

real life | relationships

> ***Practical suggestions:***
> - At your first university wedding try to get to the place early and find somewhere near by to eat; weddings are exhausting for everyone involved, make sure you're not hungry to start with.
> - When your friends get back from their honeymoon, give them a couple of days space and then phone them up and welcome them back.
> - Be prepared for life to change – relationships may still be strong, but may also be different. Allow yourself to mourn the loss of those relationships but to move on.
> - If you're worried about whether you should go and see a friend who has just got married, ask them. Don't ask for other people's opinion. Hearing something fourth-hand about what someone may or may not want is always a recipe for disaster.

we all need our mates. When your friends start getting married carry on being friends with them!

Does God provide someone for everyone?

If you do want to get married and there is no-one around who is suitable, you might ask God why. Has he really got someone for you? In the Bible God never promises us a partner. We need to lay down our desires before God, whatever they are, and ask him to do his will in our lives. It can be a struggle and that is why it is important to keep in relationship

> ### *Practical advice:*
> - Get your focus on God and off the search for a partner. Ask God to fulfil you in all that you are and in all the desires he has given you.
> - Keeping your attention first and foremost on God doesn't mean you can't actively look for someone. Jesus doesn't call us to be passive – you wouldn't sit and wait for an angel to tell you what university to go to, you'd fill in a form and apply. Be sensible, just not obsessed.
> - Don't put your life on hold waiting until you meet someone, live it now.

with people who know us well and understand the issues we face. Don't put your life on hold (see chapter 3) but, like Abram moving to a new land with no son and heir, be prepared to trust God and his plans for you. It may feel painful to obey God's calling and move to a small town where there is about as much chance of meeting a Christian mate as meeting the Loch Ness monster, but God promises that whatever we give up for him he will give back to us in abundance.

Whether you are single or married your focus needs to be on God. First and foremost you need to look to God to supply your needs and not to another person. If we become obsessed with trying to find another person who will be everything to us, then we are not allowing God to take control of our lives. We need to dream big and have a vision for our lives that is bigger than who we may or may not marry. God has plans for you and he has promised that they are bigger and better than anything you can imagine.

Dating non-Christians
If you're not going out with a non-Christian, don't start. Say you meet someone at work; he's good-looking and you feel really attracted to him; you persuade yourself that he might even become a Christian if you go out with him. But six months down the line when you really love him and want him to become a Christian and he still isn't, you will feel caught between a rock and a hard place. It is very hard to maintain a Christian faith and have a relationship with someone who doesn't believe what you believe. The Bible says, don't do it (2 Corinthians 6:14).

> **Practical advice:**
> • You will always be able to find arguments to convince yourself why going out with a non-Christian is a good idea. Share your problem with other Christians and make yourself accountable to other people.
> • If you are already going out with a non-Christian, make sure your relationship with that person isn't interfering with your relationship with God. Jesus says we need to be prepared to love him more than a partner and to lose what we see as 'our life' if we want to find life with him (Matthew 10:37–39). Anything that comes between God and us needs to be realigned. Pray with a Christian friend about that relationship and be accountable to them, especially in the physical aspect of the relationship.

Parents

You may be happy being single, but what if your parents are desperate for you to settle down so they can have have grandkids?

'Whenever I spoke to my mother she kept talking about me being single. If I ever mentioned a boy she would talk about him in the next conversation I had with her. It took me many years to realize it was her problem, not mine. In her head she was worried that if I never married I would never be independent from her and my dad. In reality I had moved away when I first started university seven years earlier and now have my own house and social life in a different city.'

Whatever your family's expectations are, don't be forced into someone else's mould. Ask God what he wants for your life and follow that.

Practical suggestions:
- If your family are dropping constant hints, have a chat with them about it and explain why you don't like their behaviour.
- If you feel you can't do it face-to-face, as they might get the wrong end of the stick, write them a letter. It's far better to confront the problem than to stop speaking to them because they are always talking about something you don't want to discuss.

real life | relationships

In brief

relationships

Whether you are single or married make sure you live your life. Don't wait around for the right person before you try and fulfil your lifelong calling.

Singleness is no less important than marriage – it's not just a stage you go through until you get married.

Being single or married doesn't make you less or more of a person – God makes you complete.

Keep your focus on God and not on the search for a partner. Ask God to fulfil you in all that you are and in all the desires he has given you.

Don't start going out with a non-Christian. If you are already going out with someone who doesn't believe the same things as you, make your relationship accountable to another Christian.

Weddings are great fun, but eat before you get there and expect an energetic day.

relationships

The wedding may be over but the marriage has only just begun, so carry on supporting your friends – they might need it during this time of adjustment.
If you don't know whether you can still pop round to your now-married friends' house – ask them! If your family won't let the 'M' subject drop, talk to them and explain how you are feeling.

Further reading
Camerin Courtney, *Table for One* (Fleming H. Revell, 2002).
Al Hsu, *The Single Issue* (Inter-Varsity Press, 1997).
Nigel Pollock, *The Relationships Revolution* (Inter-Varsity Press, 1998).

chapter 10

faith

If you were lucky enough to be part of a Christian community in your university or college or if you belonged to a church with lots of students and people of your own age, you might find it difficult when your friends leave and that close Christian support disappears. For once there aren't people who know exactly what's happening in your life; your mates no longer ask the questions that challenge you; and suddenly you realize it's just you and God in the boat, so maybe you'd better start talking!

In 1 Corinthians 3, Paul rebukes the believers for still needing milk not solid food. Paul tells them to grow up and follow Jesus Christ, instead of arguing about whether they are following Paul or Apollos. We need to make sure we are following Jesus and not our vicar or Christian Union president. We are God's temple and God's Spirit lives in us (1 Corinthians 3:16). We need to recognize this as we move away from formal support structures to new situations. Whatever happens and wherever you go, remember that God goes with you.

'After university I missed the Christian support. I was used to going to CU, house group, two prayer meetings a week and church. It sounds a bit excessive now but then I had so much time it didn't

really matter. After university I realized that it was now just me and God. I wasn't going to any prayer meetings so I had to learn to pray by myself. I was so used to praying with other people I found it really difficult to pray for a proper period of time. I still struggle but I think it has improved my relationship with God so it is now more personal and less polished.'

Another graduate writes:

'I was really involved in the chaplaincy at university and was part of an ecumenical community. I really missed it when I left especially the lack of ecumenical worship in "real life". I found the most important thing I learnt was to try new things and not merely mourn the old.'

Getting used to life being just about you and God can be hard – people enjoy corporate life and worship as they often find it easier to engage with God in a group. But at the end of the day your relationship with God is about you and God.

Your faith changes

As you grow up, your faith changes. This is a normal and healthy part of growing up. As a child you may have been able to recite every single story in the *Toddlers' Bible*, but now nothing seems as concrete as it once was. Maybe you became a Christian at university, had loads of Christian mates and life seemed great, but now you're really struggling.

'After graduating I found my faith a challenge, mostly because I was trying to sideline God and keep life for myself. He didn't let me go though and hung in there. Don't expect everything to fall into line straight away. Life's changed, it takes a while to catch up and work out who you are again.'

Don't panic, don't worry, you're not alone. Throughout the Bible we find people struggling with their faith and with God. Read the Psalms – many are good examples of people struggling with life and faith but choosing to talk to God and praise him in the midst of their pain (e.g. Psalms 31 and 42).

If you have doubts about God, life and the universe, tell him. God is big enough to cope with your fears, anxieties and questions. I remember a particularly difficult period in my life when I had had enough of God. Life was a mess and I wasn't sure he was around or even that I wanted him to be so. I told him I'd let go of the rope holding us together and that it would serve him right! As I made that decision I realized that even if I let go of God, he wouldn't let go of me. For years I had been hanging on to this rope, desperately clinging to it, afraid of what would happen if I let go. Then when I let go I didn't fall. I realized that entwined round me was another rope, a rope that was part of me. That was the rope that was connected to God not the one I had been holding on to so desperately tightly.

There's an old story of an elephant giving a monkey a lift to the market so he can sell his coconuts. The monkey is perched on the elephant's back. His hands are full of coconuts and he's trying desperately not to lose his balance. The elephant asks the monkey why he isn't holding on? The monkey replies: 'I wouldn't want you to have to carry me and my coconuts.' God is more than able to carry us and our doubts. Take your hard times to God, not away from God. Go to those around you and ask them for their wisdom and insight. Through exploring our doubts we grow in God. If we suppress our doubts, we often suppress our faith as well.

There's an example of a doubting believer in the Bible – Jesus' disciple, Thomas. Jesus had appeared to all the disciples except him and Thomas wasn't sure about this whole rising from the dead business. He told the other disciples: 'Unless I see the nail marks in his hands and put my finger where the nails were, and put my hand into his side, I will not believe' (John 20:25). Eight days later all the disciples were together and Jesus appeared, spoke to Thomas personally and said: 'Put your finger here; see my hands. Reach out your hand and put it into my side' (John 20:27).

Jesus offered him proof by sharing his scars with Thomas. He shared the moments of pain when he had felt alone and isolated from God too. And God didn't judge him but loved him. That's what God does to us when we come to him with our doubts and fears.

Faith and the future

'When I look at other people, some of them seem to have this definite calling where they know what they are doing with their life and why. It hasn't come down on a pink fluffy cloud but it's an intrinsic part of who they are which they know is from God. For me it hasn't happened like that. Does that mean my faith isn't as good or is that just the way it is?'

Don't believe the myths! Most graduates don't have a definite plan of what God wants them to do after graduation, they just hope God will lead them as they move from one thing to the next. One ex-student explains how this affected her faith:

'My faith has changed lots since university, but so have I, and I think the two are improving together. I know God's provision more and the fact that God's plan is for us to decide on something to do rather than wait for his direction. Overall this has been positive, but it felt hard at times.'

It's easy to wish that God had given us a silver envelope with our life's calling spelled out on a card inside. When that doesn't happen, what do we do? Sit around and wait for it, or move on? Sometimes it can be hard to walk ahead not knowing exactly where to step. We need to carry on walking even when we don't know the way.

God is a loving father. A father is not being responsible for his children if he tells them what to do at every turn. A good father lets his children make decisions from when they are very young. When they are still too young to have an opinion about important matters, the father may ask them what colour socks they want to wear. Children learn through this to make choices as they grow up. Sometimes they will make good choices, sometimes bad choices, but through it they learn to be their own person, not a clone of their parents. And that's how our Father God treats us, allowing us to make our own choices, but in the framework of his love and plans for us. It doesn't mean you're less of a Christian if you don't know what to do with your life; God will reveal it as you go on, and he promises that if we acknowledge him, he will direct our paths (Proverbs 3:6).

Keeping the good stuff
At university I found there was a lot of time to pray – whatever you were into, some group were praying for it. As you leave full-time education remember God still hears all your prayers, whether they are to do with third-world debt, injustice, friends, family, exams or a blocked drainpipe. Don't lose the perspective that God cares for everything including the little things in life.

'Since leaving student life I have become a lot more conscious of God's provision. I had nowhere to live, no car and was due to start a job in a week. We prayed and within the space of a week, we got both. I'm amazed by the detail God cares about. It encourages you

to pray about the big stuff. My faith is now much more based on trust rather than an emotional response in a big meeting.'

One of the best things about student life is the opportunity to discuss your faith with people who have different viewpoints. When you leave education, you lose the forum to discuss the big picture, but it doesn't mean you can't recreate it. Don't get bogged down in pointless arguments that offend those around you; instead, find time to have the big conversations that help you explore and be passionate about what you believe.

Throwing away the negative stuff

'When I look back now I cringe at how intolerant I was at college. I rammed theology down people's throats as a fierce evangelical believer. Then when I left college I went completely the other way and decided God didn't care about individual morals but the world as a whole. Both times I was trying to fit God into the box I had made for him, instead of letting him be God. The two were part of a journey and I feel like I have learnt from both the liberal and evangelical ends of the spectrum.'

Sometimes we can allow our enthusiasm to dwarf our wisdom. When I first came to Leeds in the late 90s it was very trendy to shout when you prayed, and I don't just mean praying loudly but actually shouting so that the rest of the campus could hear. There was nothing actually wrong with that, but it wasn't a direct heaven-sent command that the whole of the university had to hear our prayers. It is important to re-evaluate what is of God and what is actually fashionable Christianity.

Take your faith back to the Bible and look at who God is. Then in relationship with other Christians explore your faith together and find out who Jesus really is. Let God take the lead, don't let your own prejudices guide you. Trust God to reveal himself to you – your faith may seem quite different from your neighbour's faith, but you can only see the outside, God sees the heart.

Listen to others. Be prepared to accept criticism and in humility consider whether other people are right. They may not be, but then again they might be. Ask God for his perspective.

Finally

As you leave student life and your faith changes, don't assume you have it all right now. In ten years' time you may look back and think how naïve you were when you first left school or when you graduated. Don't be cynical about other people's faith and how they express their relationship with God, instead look at your own faith and make sure in the day-to-day living you don't lose your passion and excitement for Jesus. Make sure you take the plank out of your own eye before starting on the speck in someone else's (Matthew 7:3–5).

Finally, keep encouraging your friends from school or university, wherever they are in their faith. Look around at work or at church for relationships that will challenge you, maybe people who are in the same sphere of work who you could meet up with once a month to talk about relevant issues. Remember to serve those around you and be an example of Jesus to each person that you meet.

real life | faith

In brief

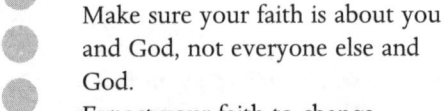

Make sure your faith is about you and God, not everyone else and God.

Expect your faith to change.

Don't be afraid to have doubts – God can cope!

God won't necessarily tell you exactly what to do with your life. But don't panic!

Hold on to what is positive about your faith.

Use your friends and the Bible to question what might be fashion rather than God in your Christian life.

Don't allow yourself to be cynical about those behind or before you. Be an encourager and an encouragement.

Further reading
Philip Jensen and Tony Payne, *Guidance and the Voice of God* (Matthias Media, 1997).

postscript

a confession

I still find growing up is a difficult process and although I try, I find it hard to take my own advice. I'm not great at being generous, nor am I great at having a good work–home balance. But I continue to try and only in trying can I become more like the person God made me to be.

Through writing this book and talking to other people about their faith and how it has changed since they left education behind, I have allowed myself time to think and contemplate on our relationships with God. At university we were all pretty much like peas in a pod, now we vary much more as life continues to chip away at us making us into different and unique people. When I was a child I remember looking at my teachers and wondering; 'What do they worry about?' Adult life seemed much calmer away from homework and exams. But as you get older, life doesn't get easier. Instead loved ones in your families die, couples separate, friends and family suffer infertility and miscarriage, and some the indignity of debilitating illness. At times you feel like joining in with the writer of Ecclesiastes and shouting 'Everything is meaningless' (Ecclesiastes 1:2).

Yet throughout the struggles, the pain and the questions I have to conclude there is no other way. Indeed although there are not even answers to our questions we still need to carry on with a steady plodding forward. Labour, wisdom, folly and wealth mean nothing on their own, but when we put our hand in the hand of God we are safer than on a known path and God promises to guide us on to the end.

for further thought...

This final section provides questions and reflections to help you think through issues arising from this book. It can be worked through on your own or in small groups.

1. Preparing for change
(See chapters 1 and 2 of this book.)

When I didn't get the grades I needed for the university course I had applied for, I felt really low and unsure of what to do with my life – I'd even applied for a job as a postal worker. Then I got a phone call from the university saying there was a spare place. It was one week before term started. My mum went into panic mode; we hadn't bought anything for going away and suddenly there were just days until I was making a 200-mile journey from Bristol to Leeds. I was working at a garden centre to earn some cash and I remember coming back to my bedroom after a particularly hot September day to find a whole load of thermal underwear on my bed. My mum

real life | for further thought...

was convinced I was going to freeze to death in a 'northern' city.

Thinking about what we might need, both spiritually and physically, can help us prepare for changes ahead. I'm one of those people who like to know exactly what's happening, and when. Unfortunately, life doesn't often turn out like that. Jesus knew that, which is why, from the very start of his ministry, he began preparing his disciples for the day when he would leave them.

One day Jesus asked his disciples who they thought he was and Simon Peter answered: 'You are the Christ, the Son of the living God' (Matthew 16:16). It's an inspired answer and Simon probably revels in Jesus' response without listening to the second half of what he is saying as Jesus explains that he must suffer and die for God's purposes to be accomplished.

Change can often be stressful, and difficult times were ahead for Simon Peter. Later on we will find him fearful and afraid, the inspired confession of Christ a distant memory.

Action point
Make a list of all the good stuff God has done in your life, especially over the last few years while you have been a student. Keep it somewhere safe so that you can refer back to it in difficult times ahead.

Peter gets it wrong in Matthew 16:21–28. Jesus is trying to explain to the disciples that the dark times ahead were part of God's plan when Peter rebukes Jesus and says 'Never Lord, this shall never happen to you.' Peter didn't see the big picture and instead tried to hold Jesus back from God's will.

Action point

Look at your life and priorities to see if there is anything that is holding you back from God's will or from the exciting future God has planned for you. For example, it may be fear of the unknown or a relationship that needs healing. Pray about these issues and ask God for his courage to follow him even when things get tough. Could you share these issues with a friend and write some accountability questions for them to ask you?

Peter may have been rebuked by Jesus but Jesus never gave up on Peter. If you have friends who you have agreed to be accountable to, you must make sure you do not give up on those relationships when you are held to account. Jesus may have called Peter 'Satan', but Peter continued to be in relationship with him. In Matthew 17 Jesus shares a special experience with John, James and Peter, as they see Jesus transfigured, his face shining like the sun and his clothes becoming dazzling white. This is a faith-strengthening encounter which the disciples would remember in the days after Jesus' death.

Action point

Go back to the list you made for the first action point. Why not write a letter to yourself or to a friend, itemizing all the good things God has done for you as a reminder of God's goodness? Put it in a place where you will see it in a year's time (such as the back of a diary) or look on the internet for a site that can email it to you at a future date.

In the latter part of Matthew 26 Jesus warned the disciples of the difficulties ahead and urged them to pray in preparation. They insisted that they could cope; Peter said, 'Even if I have to die with you, I will never disown you.' But when Jesus encouraged them to pray, they fell asleep.

Action point

Write a list of issues you are likely to come across in the next few months or years. What steps can you take now to minimize their effects? (For example, if you have an issue with your parents but are planning on moving back home, how can you make the relationship with your parents better? Maybe you could phone home more frequently or go and visit them?)

Sometimes when change happens we don't deal with it very well. Peter was trying to help, but if you really wanted to attack someone and leave them unable to arrest your master you wouldn't cut off their ear (John 18:3–12)!

Action point

Pray about the issue of change and your response to it with those you are accountable to and give them some questions they can ask you in the weeks and months to come so that you can deal with change a bit more effectively than Peter did in this passage.

Finally, the most important thing to remember is that God is with you in everything that is going to happen. We are his children whom he loves and delights in. Simon Peter had a mixture of ups and downs and even denied Jesus three times, but Jesus always carried on loving him and even gave him the important job of building his new kingdom. No matter how many times we fail, God can, and wants to, use us again.

2. Who am I in God?

(See chapters 3, 4 and 9 of this book.)

Things people say to us can really hurt. I remember being told not to apply for the school choir when I was eleven. For years after I was embarrassed about my singing; you'd never have caught me singing in a small group of people, or in a karaoke session. In my first job I once voiced an ambition to be a *Blue Peter* presenter only to be told scathingly by my boss, 'You could never do that, you can't even talk properly.' The great thing is that when God looks at me he doesn't wince when I sing out of tune, he doesn't even mind when I don't pronounce my 'th's properly, he looks at me and says, 'Wow, this is a child of mine who is amazing because I made her that way.'

Society often tries to define us by our job description, but God never does. He looks at us as something far more fascinating, complex and beautiful than what we do on a nine-to-five basis. As a child I always wanted one of those dolls where the skirts fold over and you have two heads – a Cinderella in rags at one end, but flip the skirt over the original head and you have a beautiful princess at the other end. Often that's how we see ourselves. We are either successful and happy (if everything is going well) or sad and unwanted (if we lose our job, our partner or our security). God sees us as much more than this, he sees all the gifts, abilities and creativity we have inside us.

Look at 1 Peter 2 verse 9 again: Peter says we are a people 'belonging to God', special and precious.

real life | for further thought ...

Action point
Reflect on the words that help us to know we are special to God. Think of the five most important people in your life. Write down a list of words you associate with them.

In work situations there may be times when you do not feel precious, maybe you have shown loyalty to a company but they have passed over you giving promotion to the next person in line. God doesn't do that to us, we belong to him and he wants us to spend time with him because we are precious.

Read Psalm 139
This psalm was written by David, a man whose life runs like a soap opera. The story opens with a rags-to-riches plot; small shepherd boy slays evil giant. Then he nearly gets murdered a few times before becoming king. Once in the palace David gets lazy and doesn't go out to fight with his army; instead he commits adultery and then murder. Reading this, you might think that he is one of the bad guys of the Bible, but in fact he is the only person who is called 'a man after God's own heart'. This psalm shows us that, despite all David's failings, he knew that God loved him.

Action point
Write the words from the previous action point and your thoughts from Psalm 139 on a sheet of paper and stick it on your fridge or somewhere you will see it. Use it to remind yourself how precious you are to God.

Belonging to God carries a responsibility. 1 Peter 2:9 says we are chosen as royal priests. Priests are people who intercede between God and man. This is what Abraham does in Genesis 18:16–33. God wants us to be part of his kingdom coming on earth. He gives us the privilege of being involved in his plan. He calls us to his own special work. Regardless of whether we are married or single, employed or unemployed, he has work for us to do.

Action point

God has a job for everyone to do: who can you intercede for? Start praying for them now! Ask a friend to hold you accountable for that commitment. As well as interceding, the priests helped people find God by being an attracting force, drawing people to God. How can you be an attracting force to those around you who do not know God? Maybe you could drop someone a card, make a cake, or visit an elderly person on your street?

We are also called to be a holy nation. In stressful times it is often easy to stop spending time with God, we are tired and choose to watch television instead of reading the Bible or praying. Maybe we are in a place where we know few people and have little accountability?

Paul says it is not enough for us to look nice on the outside, we need to be Christ-like on the inside.

Action point

Write a list of those areas in your life where you have not been holy, maybe bad habits or addictions.

Confess these to God and give them to him: he is faithful and just and will forgive you. If appropriate, share your list with a friend or trusted person who can pray for you and to whom you can be accountable.

After laying down our 'old clothes' Paul presents us with a whole new wardrobe, clothes that will make us more like Jesus (Colossians 3:1–7).

Action point

Look at verses 12–14: what attributes are missing from your life? Write a list and give examples of when you haven't acted like Jesus. Look round your house and find an object to be a visual reminder of your desire to develop those areas in your life. For example, if you are most likely to be impatient waiting for your housemate to finish using the shower, maybe you could write 'patience' on your shower gel. A piece of jewellery might be a good reminder if it is an issue you struggle with continuously during the day.

Finally, God loves us as we are but he also calls us to be more like him. Find your identity from God and ask him to shape your life so that you become more like the person he has called you to be.

3. Lifestyle issues

(*See chapters 5, 6, 7 and 8 of this book.*)

Sometimes we can pigeon-hole God into Sundays and times when we are with other Christians. But Jesus calls us to have a kingdom-lifestyle, living our lives with him day in, day out.

Running a youth group has many memorable moments, and one of my greatest frustrations is trying to get the kids to take responsibility for their actions. One week I was talking to a couple of the girls about their behaviour and problems we had experienced at that week's session. After blaming the boys, her parents, school and exams, thirteen-year-old Kerry was running out of excuses. Finally she looked up from biting her nails and said: 'It's not my fault, it's my hormones.'

How we live out life impacts those around us. The question is not 'Are you saved?' but 'Are you being saved?' Our relationship with God is an ongoing journey and we have to walk continually with God.

What has God called you to do? In Jonah 1:1–17 Jonah knew what his calling was but chose to ignore it. As a result, things were getting out of control and before he knew it he was in trouble, thrown in the sea and swallowed by a fish.

Action point

What's going on in your life? Draw a spider diagram on a big piece of paper of all the things you do with your time: work, study, leisure, etc. In another colour write down things which God has told you to do but which you are not doing: e.g. being patient at work, not making sarcastic comments in a team meeting, doing voluntary work or praying with a friend.

real life | for further thought . . .

Jonah had other plans, he didn't want to go to Nineveh and so was running away from God. However, when trouble came he turned to God and asked for his help. God helped him out and then asked him again to go to Nineveh (Jonah 2:1–10 and 3:1–9).

Action point

God never gives up on us even when we don't do what he asks us to. Pray about the issues raised in the previous action point and spend some time listening to God, asking him to speak to you. You might find it helpful to listen to some worship music or read a favourite bit of the Bible. Look out for bits that seem to jump out at you and write them down on your spider diagram.

Jonah was angry at God for having compassion on the people of Nineveh, but God loved the people more than Jonah's pride. He uses a vine to get the message home to Jonah that he is a God who cares for his people. Jonah was preaching hell, fire and brimstone without God's love and mercy. He had an important lesson to learn – that God loved those around him as much as God loved him (Jonah 3:9 and 4:1–11). God cares about the poor, both the spiritually poor and the physically poor.

Action point

Are you using your time and money to bless the poor around you? How are you using your time and money? Think of all your money, not just your 'tithe'. Is your spending righteous? What are you investing in?

Don't just think of financial investments; are you investing in people, in worthy projects? Add these to your spider diagram so you have a more holistic picture of your life.

Finally, using the 'big picture' you have created, pray about issues that arise from it. Do you need to re-align some of your priorities to do the things God has called you to do? What issues may result from this? Write a vision statement based on your spider diagram and carry it with you in your wallet. Review how you are doing every three months and pray with a friend or accountability partner about how to involve God in your whole lifestyle.